Intermediate Language Lessons

Second Book in the Lost Classics English Series

BY

EMMA SERL

TEACHER, NORMAL TRAINING SCHOOL

KANSAS CITY, MISSOURI

AND

AUTHOR OF *PRIMARY LANGUAGE LESSONS*

LOST CLASSICS BOOK COMPANY

PUBLISHER

LAKE WALES

FLORIDA

PUBLISHER'S NOTE

Recognizing the need to return to more traditional principles in education, Lost Classics Book Company is republishing forgotten late 19th and early 20th century literature and textbooks to aid parents in the education of their children.

This edition of *Intermediate Language Lessons* was reprinted from the 1914 copyright edition. The text has been updated and edited only where necessary.

This is the second book in the Lost Classics English Series, for students aged 9 through 12, following Emma Serl's *Primary Language Lessons* and preceding *Advanced Language Lessons* (based on *Aldine Third Language Book*, by Frank Spaulding, Catherine Bryce, and Huber Beuhler).

Intermediate Language Lessons has been assigned a reading level of 760L. More information concerning this reading level assessment may be obtained by visiting www.lexile.com.

© Copyright 1996
Lost Classics Book Company
Ninth Printing, September 2016

Library of Congress Catalog Card Number: 96-77553
ISBN 978-0-9652735-7-2

PREFACE

THE purpose of this book is to aid pupils to speak and write the English language correctly.

The book is intended especially for use of pupils in the fourth, fifth and sixth grades. It may, however, be adjusted to suit different conditions found in more advanced classes. If *Primary Language Lessons* was used in the last half of the second grade and through the third, the pupil is well prepared to begin *Intermediate Language Lessons*, in the fourth grade.

Attention is called to the following features: Literature studies, not only in poetry, but also in fine prose selections. Letter writing on subjects that appeal to child life, and including simple forms of business letters. Drill on correct forms of speech and words often misused. Many exercises to increase the pupil's vocabulary. The making of outlines, and writing and talking from outlines. The various forms in composition, including description, narration, conversation, dialogue, debate, and the writing of rhymes. Both reproduction and original work in oral and written composition. Sequence and careful graduation in arrangement of lessons. The careful treatment of capitalization and punctuation. Observation lessons which furnish material for talking and writing. Lessons on civic subjects, such as the school, the court, the state, cleanliness of streets, and needed improvements.

The oral composition in connection with the observation lessons not only aid the pupil in telling readily and accurately what he has seen, but give him self-possession and train him to logical thought.

When an essential fact is taught, the pupil is given practice in using the fact again and again, through dictation, reproduction, and original composition.

Thanks are due to authors and publishers for use of the following copyright material: Helen Keller and Doubleday, Page and Company, for the extract from *The Story of My Life*; Little, Brown, and Company, for two poems by Helen Hunt Jackson, and one by Dr. E. E. Hale; Dana Estes and Company for two poems by Susan Hartley Swett; *Our Dumb Animals*, for *The Horse's Prayer*; Educational Publishing Company, for *The Music of Labor*; *The Outlook*, for *The Footpath to Peace*, by Dr. Van Dyke; Whitaker and Ray-Wiggin Company, for *Columbus*, by Joaquin Miller. The selections from Longfellow, Whittier, Lowell, Holmes, Alice and Phoebe Cary, Lucy Larcom, Celia Thaxter, J. G. Saxe, and Frank D. Sherman are used by permission of and special arrangement with Houghton Mifflin Company.

CONTENTS

PART ONE

vi CONTENTS

LESSON PAGE

32. CONVERSATION—FRUITS..33
33. DESCRIPTION—A FRUIT STORE....................................34
34. CORRECT USE OF WORDS 35
35. SELECTION FOR STUDY—THE BAREFOOT BOY 36
36. CONVERSATION—THE FARMER 39
37. POSSESSIVE FORM 40
38. COMPOSITION 41
39. NAMES 41
40. SELECTION FOR STUDY—STORY OF THE FLAX.................42
41. COMPOSITION—DESCRIPTION 44
42. COMPOSITION—THE THIRSTY CROW.............................44
43. COMPOSITION—DIALOGUE 45
44. CONVERSATION—THE CAT FAMILY 46
45. COMPOSITION—DESCRIPTION OF AN ANIMAL 47
46. DICTATION—DESCRIPTION OF A LION..........................48
47. REPRODUCTION—A FABLE 49
48. COMPOSITION 50
49. REPRODUCTION—A FABLE 51
50. IMAGINATIVE LETTER..51
51. SUMMARY 52
52. DICTATION—QUOTATION MARKS 53
53. MEANING OF WORDS..54
54. SELECTION FOR STUDY—DON'T GIVE UP 55
55. CONTRACTIONS 56
56. QUOTATIONS..57
57. DICTATION..58
58. CORRECT USE OF WORDS 58
59. DESCRIPTION OF A GAME...59
60. LETTER WRITING..59
61. PICTURE STUDY—GAMBOLS OF CHILDREN 60
62. CORRECT USE OF WORDS 62
63. THE COMMA IN ADDRESS...63
64. ORAL COMPOSITION—A STORY...................................64
65. SELECTION FOR STUDY—THE VILLAGE BLACKSMITH...........65
66. HENRY WADSWORTH LONGFELLOW..............................68
67. SINGULAR AND PLURAL FORMS 69
68. SELECTION FOR STUDY—THE WIND AND THE MOON...........71
69. CONVERSATION—CLOTHING 74

CONTENTS

vii

CONTENTS

CONTENTS

PART THREE

CONTENTS

CONTENTS

CONTENTS

From a painting by Delaroche
THE FINDING OF MOSES

PART ONE

LESSON 1

SELECTION FOR STUDY

THE FINDING OF MOSES

Many hundred years ago, in the land of Egypt, a Hebrew mother placed her baby boy in a tiny boat made of bulrushes and hid him among the reeds by the riverside. She did this because Pharaoh, the king of the country, had ordered that all the Hebrew baby boys should be killed. The mother left the child hidden there, while his sister Miriam stood far-off to watch.

At about noon the daughter of Pharaoh went down to the river to bathe. As she and her maids walked slowly along the bank, they saw the boat among the rushes. Wondering what it could be, the princess bade one of her maids to bring it to her.

There in the boat of bulrushes they found the baby boy. When he cried, the king's daughter had compassion on him and said, "This is one of the Hebrews' children."

Then said his sister Miriam to the princess, "Shall I go and call a nurse of the Hebrew women, that she may nurse the child for thee?"

1

And the king's daughter said to her, "Go."

The sister ran quickly and called the baby's mother.

Pharaoh's daughter said to the mother, "Take the child and nurse it for me, and I will pay thee thy wages."

After the child had grown larger, he went to live with the king's daughter as her son. She called his name Moses, for she said, "I drew him out of the water."

1. Read the story and tell it.
2. Describe the picture.

LESSON 2

NAMES OF PERSONS AND PLACES

1. From the story, "The Finding of Moses," copy:
   A. The name of the baby
   B. The name of the baby's sister
   C. The name of the king

2. With what kind of letter does the name of a person or place begin?

3. Make a rule for this use of the capital letter.

4. Write the names of—

   A. two countries   D. four cities
   B. five boys   E. two states
   C. two celebrated men   F. five girls

LESSON 3

SELECTION FOR STUDY

THE STONE IN THE ROAD

There was once a king who lived in a beautiful palace near a little village. He loved the people in the village and tried in many ways to help them.

But the people were selfish and did not try to help one another. The good king wished to teach them a lesson, so he arose early one morning and placed a large stone in the road which led past his palace. Then, hiding himself nearby, he watched to see what would happen.

Soon a woman came along driving some goats to pasture. She scolded because the stone was in the way, and stepping over it she went on up the road.

By and by a man came, riding a donkey. He complained about the stone but drove around it and went on his way.

Other people came and went. Each remarked about the stone, but no one tried to move it.

At last, when the day was almost ended, the miller's boy came down the road. Seeing the stone he halted and put down the bundle he was carrying.

"This stone should not be here," he said. "Someone might fall over it. I will move it out of the way."

The stone was heavy, and the boy could scarcely lift it. But by repeated efforts he at last pushed it from its place and rolled it to one side. As he turned to continue on his way, he saw that in the place where the stone had been there was a bag upon which something was written. Bending closer he read these words: "This bag of gold belongs to the one who helps others by removing the stone from the road."

The miller's boy carried his treasure homeward with a happy heart, and as the king returned to his palace he said, "I am glad that I have found someone who is unselfish enough to think of the comfort of others."

1. Tell the story, from the following outline:

    A. The king
    B. The people
    C. The stone in the road
    D. The people who passed
    E. The miller's boy
    F. The bag of gold

2. Read, in the last part of the story, what the king said.

3. With what kind of letter is the word *I* always written?

4. Make a rule for this use of the capital letter.

LESSON 4

SELECTION TO BE MEMORIZED

True worth is in being, not seeming;
    In doing each day that goes by
Some little good; not in the dreaming
    Of great things to do by and by.
For whatever men say in their blindness,
    And spite of the fancies of youth,
There's nothing so kingly as kindness,
    And nothing so royal as truth.

—ALICE CARY

1. Copy the quotation and memorize it.

LESSON 5

COMPOSITION—A PRINCE STORY

1. Read the story, "The Stone in the Road," then make a similar story about a prince and a beautiful jewel. The prince places the jewel in a bucket far down in a deep well, then he dresses himself up as a poor old man and asks all who pass to draw water for him to drink.
2. Make an outline of your story.
3. Tell the story from the outline.
4. Begin your story in this way: Once upon a time, a prince _____.

LESSON 6

SELECTION FOR STUDY

THE WISE FAIRY

Once, in a rough wild country,
  On the other side of the sea,
There lived a dear little fairy,
  And her home was in a tree;
A dear little, wise little fairy,
  And as rich as she could be.

To northward and to southward,
  She could overlook the land,
And that was why she had her house
  In a tree, you understand.
For she was the friend of the friendless,
  And her heart was in her hand.

And when she saw poor women
  Patiently, day by day,
Spinning, spinning, and spinning
  Their lonesome lives away,
She would hide in the flax of their distaffs
  A lump of gold, they say.

And when she saw poor ditchers,
  Knee-deep in some wet dike,
Digging, digging, and digging,

To their very graves, belike,
She would hide a shining lump of gold
Where their spades would be sure to strike.

And when she saw poor children
   Their goats from the pastures take,
Or saw them milking and milking,
   Till their arms were ready to break,
What a splashing in their milking pails
   Her gifts of gold would make!

Sometimes, in the night, a fisher
   Would hear her sweet low call,
And all at once a salmon of gold
   Right out of his net would fall;
But what I have to tell you
   Is the strangest thing of all.

If any ditcher, or fisher,
   Or child, or spinner old,
Bought shoes for his feet, or bread to eat,
   Or a coat to keep from the cold,
The gift of the good old fairy
   Was always trusty gold.

But if a ditcher, or a fisher,
   Or a spinner, or child so gay,
Bought jewels, or wine, or silks so fine,
   Or staked his pleasure at play,

The fairy's gold in his very hold
Would turn to a lump of clay.

So, by and by, the people
Got open their stupid eyes:
"We must learn to spend to some good end,"
They said, "if we are wise;
'Tis not in the gold we waste or hold,
That a golden blessing lies."

—ALICE CARY

1. Explain the third stanza.
2. What is a *distaff*?
3. Explain the seventh stanza.
4. Explain the eighth stanza.
5. Tell the story of the wise fairy.
6. Who wrote this poem?
7. What lesson did the author wish to teach?
8. Which part of the poem do you like best?

LESSON 7

ORAL COMPOSITION

Frank and May Rogers each received two dollars for a Christmas present. Tell a story showing how one of the children spent the money foolishly, and one wisely.

LESSON 8

THE SENTENCE

A. A fairy lived on the other side of the sea.
B. Where did she hide lumps of gold?
C. Do not spend gold foolishly.

1. Which of the groups of words tells something?
   Note: A group of words that tells something is a *statement*.
2. What mark of punctuation is placed after a statement?
3. Which of the groups of words asks something?
   Note: A group of words that asks something is a *question*.
4. What mark of punctuation is placed after a question?
5. Which of the groups of words makes a command?
   Note: A group of words that orders something is a *command*.
   Note: A group of words that tells, or asks, or commands is a *sentence*.
6. With what kind of letter does the first word of every sentence begin?
7. Write five statements about "The Wise Fairy."
8. Write five questions about "The Wise Fairy."

From a painting by J. G. Brown
THE FLOWER GIRL

9. Write five commands that the fairy might have given to the people, or that they may have given to each other.

LESSON 9

PICTURE STUDY—THE FLOWER GIRL

1. What story does the picture tell?
2. How old do you think the little girl is?
3. From what kind of a home do you imagine she may have come?
4. Why do you think she is selling flowers?
5. What do you think the boys are saying?
6. Do you imagine that they will buy any flowers?
7. How do you think these boys make money?
8. Can you suggest another name for the picture?

LESSON 10

COMPOSITION

1. Write the story that one of the boys in the picture, *The Flower Girl*, might tell his sister. Begin it in this way:
   As I was going down the street I _____.

LESSON 11

USE OF THE DICTIONARY

1. How are words in the dictionary arranged?
2. How is the pronunciation of a word indicated?
3. Write words containing the following sounds:
   a ā ä e ē i ī ȯ ō u̇ ü ə ᵊ ȯi au̇ ŋ
4. Study in your dictionary the following:

hedge	mirror	meadow	compassion
flax	refer	dictation	paragraph
shelter	stanza	powerful	description
brim	initial	orchard	

5. Copy the words, dividing them into syllables and placing marks of pronunciation as given in the dictionary. Pronounce the words.

LESSON 12

CORRECT USE OF WORDS

A. Did you call him?
B. Did you call me?
C. Did you call him and me?
D. Mother bought some candy for you.
E. Mother bought some candy for me.
F. Mother bought some candy for you and me.

1. Study the sentences.
2. Write a sentence containing the word *me*.
3. Write the sentence again, using *him* and *me* in place of *me*.
4. Write another sentence containing the word *me*.
5. Write the sentence again, using *you* and *me* in place of *me*.
6. Write another sentence containing *me*.
7. Write the sentence again, using *her* and *me* in place of *me*.
8. Write a sentence containing the word *us*.
9. Write the sentence again, using *them* and *us* in place of *us*.

LESSON 13

SELECTION TO BE MEMORIZED

THE ROBIN

In the tall elm tree sat the robin bright,
    Through the rainy April day,
And he caroled clear with a pure delight,
    In the face of the sky so gray.
And the silver rain through the blossoms dropped,
    And fell on the robin's coat,
And his brave red breast, but he never stopped
    Piping his cheerful note.

For oh, the fields were green and glad,
    And the blissful life that stirred
In the earth's wide breast, was full and warm
    In the heart of the little bird.
The rain cloud lifted, the sunset light
    Streamed wide over valley and hill;
As the plains of heaven the land grew bright,
    And the warm south wind was still.

Then loud and clear called the happy bird,
    And rapturously he sang,
Till wood and meadow and riverside
    With jubilant echoes rang.
But the sun dropped down in the quiet west,
    And he hushed his song at last;
All nature softly sank to rest,
    And the April day had passed.

                    —CELIA THAXTER

1. Find in the dictionary words that might be used for *caroled, piping, blissful, rapturously, jubilant.*
2. Which do you like better, the words you found in the dictionary or the ones the author uses?
   Note: A single line of poetry is called a verse.
   Note: The parts into which a poem is divided are called stanzas.
3. With what kind of letter does the first word of each line of a poem begin?

LESSON 14

CORRECT USE OF WORDS

1. Copy the following sentences, filling the blanks with *is* or *are*:

   A. There _____ a tall elm tree in the meadow.
   B. There _____ a robin in the tree.
   C. There _____ green fields nearby.
   D. There _____ rain clouds in the sky.
   E. There _____ a warm wind blowing from the south.

2. Copy the sentences again, filling the blanks with *was* or *were*.

3. Use in sentences: *is, are, was, were.*

4. Begin each sentence with *There.*

LESSON 15

CONVERSATION—BIRDS

A. quail	F. meadowlark	K. owl
B. bluebird	G. oriole	L. swan
C. goldfinch	H. flicker	M. duck
D. heron	I. hawk	N. woodpecker
E. stork	J. crane	O. sparrow

1. Which of these birds are swimmers?
2. What kind of feet have they?

3. Which of these birds have long legs and wade in the water?
4. Which are birds of prey? What kind of bills have they?
5. Which are seed eaters?
6. Which are sweet singers?
7. Tell what you can of the habits of these birds.

LESSON 16

COMPOSITION—DESCRIPTION OF A BIRD

I am thinking of a bird that is not as large as the robin. Its colors are orange and black. It eats bugs and worms. It weaves its nest, hanging the nest in a tall tree. It sings sweetly.

1. Of what bird am I thinking?
2. Write a similar description of one of the birds mentioned in Lesson 15, or of some other bird that you have seen.

Follow this outline in writing:

A. Size	D. Nest
B. Color	E. Song
C. Food	F. Other habits

3. Read your description aloud, and let the rest of the class guess the answer.

LESSON 17

CORRECT USE OF WORDS

1. Write three sentences telling about what you have taught a dog or other pet to do.

2. Write three sentences telling what you have learned at school.

3. Write two sentences telling something you have learned outside of school.

4. Write a sentence telling what birds teach their young.

5. When is it correct to use the word *learn?*

6. When is it correct to use the word *teach?*

7. Use in sentences the following: *this bird, that bird, these birds, those birds.*

8. Which of the sentences refer to birds *near* you?

9. Which sentences refer to birds *away from* you?

10. Which of the sentences refer to *one* bird?

11. Which refer to *more than one* bird?

12. Make a rule for the use of *this, that, these, those.*

LESSON 18

SELECTION FOR STUDY

THE RED-HEADED WOODPECKER

The pair of Redheads had spent a whole month in the spring picking out a new home, for they were a young couple and had never kept house before. The new home was a large, clean, comfortable hole, about a foot and a half deep, in a dying oak.

The oak had been chosen because it was near a house, for they remembered that the people living there had often thrown them food during the summer before; and surely food which they would not have to dig for was worth considering.

They were a long time in digging out their home, but they had enjoyed the work even though it was hard. They had taken turn about, each working some twenty minutes.

When the house was finished, the birds were delighted with it, and it certainly was a snug little place. To human creatures on the ground below, it looked like nothing more than a large auger hole; but if they had taken the trouble to climb up, they would have found the cleanest pocket of a home that they had ever seen.

In it six little ones were hatched and cared for. It was astonishing how much those nestlings ate. The parents fed them insects, some of which they caught on their sticky tongues as they flew through the air, and some they had to get under bark on dead trees. These insects they drew out with the sawlike edges of their tongues.

—FROM *OUR BIRDS AND THEIR NESTLINGS*

1. Tell something of the red-headed woodpecker.
2. What other birds build nests in holes which they make in the sides of trees?
3. How does a woodpecker cling to the side of a tree?
4. This story is divided into five parts. The first part tells about the home of the woodpeckers.
   A. What does the second part tell about?
   B. The third part? C. The fourth? D. The fifth?

Note: Each of these parts is called a *paragraph*. Paragraphs are composed of one or more sentences referring to the same central thought. Notice that the first word of each paragraph is set a little to the right of the margin. The first word of each paragraph is said to be *indented*.

LESSON 19

AN IMAGINARY DIALOGUE

Robin and Mrs. Robin are trying to find a place for a nest. Robin wishes to build in the elm tree near the barn; Mrs. Robin says she is afraid of the cat. Robin suggests some other place, but Mrs. Robin does not like it. Mrs. Robin finds a branch in the maple tree that suits her. They begin to build the nest. Mrs. Robin brings some horsehair, and Robin finds a few pieces of string.

1. Write in dialogue form an imaginary conversation between the two.
   Use this form:

   Robin: _____ _____ _____.
   Mrs. Robin: _____ _____ _____.
   Robin: _____ _____ _____.

LESSON 20

WORDS OF A SERIES

A. The canary and the meadowlark and the oriole and the bluebird can sing.

B. The canary, the meadowlark, the oriole, and the bluebird can sing.

Note: The names of birds in sentences A and B are said to be in *series*.

1. What word connects the names in A?
2. Where are commas used in B?
3. What punctuation mark separates words of a series, when not all the connecting words are expressed?
4. Write a sentence stating four things that a robin can do.
5. Write a sentence containing the names of five kinds of animals.
6. Write a sentence containing the names of five kinds of fruit trees.
7. Write a sentence mentioning any six objects.
8. Write a sentence containing the names of the colors of the rainbow.
9. Write a sentence containing the names of three of the states.

Note: Do not use *and* more than once in any sentence.

LESSON 21

PARAGRAPHS

Arrange the following sentences into four paragraphs; be sure that each paragraph contains sentences referring to one central thought:

AN INDIAN LEGEND

A priest went forth in the early dawn.

The sky was clear.

The grass and the flowers waved in the breeze that rose as the sun threw its beams over the earth.

Birds of all kinds vied with each other, as they sang their joy on that glorious morning.

The priest stood listening.

Suddenly, off at one side, he heard a trill that rose higher and clearer than all the rest.

He moved toward the place whence the song came, that he might see what manner of bird it was that could send farther than all the others its happy notes.

As he came near, he beheld a tiny brown bird with open bill, the feathers on its throat rippling with the fervor of its song.

It was the wren, the smallest, the least powerful of birds, that seemed to be most glad, and to pour out in melody to the rising sun its delight in life.

As the priest looked, he thought: "Here is a teaching for my people.

"Everyone can be happy; even the weakest can have his song of thanks."

So he told to his people the story of the wren, and it has been handed down from that day—a day so long ago that no man can remember the time.

—FROM *OUR BIRDS AND THEIR NESTLINGS*

LESSON 22

CONVERSATION—INDIANS

1. Tell what you can of the following:
   A. Indian homes
   B. Occupations of the men
   C. Occupations of the women
   D. Education of the boys
   E. Wigwams
   F. Canoes
   G. Weapons
   H. Food—how prepared
2. Bring to school Indian relics, or pictures of Indian life.

LESSON 23

COMPOSITION—INDIANS

1. Write a short composition about Indians. Follow the outline given in Lesson 22. Begin the composition in this way:

Long before the white people came to America, Indians roamed here and there over this broad country.

LESSON 24

TITLES AND ABBREVIATIONS

A. President Adams   D. Admiral Evans
B. Doctor Johnson   E. Judge Fuller
C. Uncle George   F. Cousin Ada

1. With what kind of letter does a title begin when it is written with the name of a person?
2. Make a rule for this use of the capital letter.
Note: Words are sometimes written in a shorter way; they are then said to be *abbreviated*.

3. Write the names of the months and their abbreviations.
4. Write the names of the days of the week and their abbreviations.
5. Write the name of the state in which you live and its abbreviation.
6. With what kind of letter does the name of each day of the week and month of the year begin? What punctuation mark follows an abbreviation? Write the names for which the following abbreviations stand:

A. Rev.　　C. Ave.　　E. Jr.　　G. Mr..
B. Dr.　　　D. St.　　　F. Sr.　　H. Mrs.

LESSON 25

HELEN KELLER

On the third day of May, 1880, a baby girl was born, who has since become known to the world as Helen Keller. The baby was pretty and bright, but before she was old enough to talk she had a dreadful illness which left her both blind and deaf.

For nearly six years she was very sad and lonely, for she could neither see nor hear nor talk. Then a wonderful teacher came, who began to spell words into Helen's hand. The child imitated the signs, but for some time she did not know that her teacher was trying to talk to her. When at last she understood that she could communicate with people, she was greatly excited. Every day she learned the names of new things, and in a short time she could spell out whole sentences on her fingers.

By placing her fingers upon the lips and throat of her teacher she even learned to speak aloud. Her progress was rapid, and after completing her high school studies she went to college. She is now a graduate of one of the largest universities, and she has shown the world how one can be happy and useful, even though greatly afflicted.

1. Why is Helen Keller's teacher called wonderful?
2. Tell the story of Helen Keller.
3. Find out anything else you can about her.
4. What is the *central* thought in each paragraph of the selection?
5. Use the following words in sentences: *A. communicate B. imitate C. graduate.*
6. Can you find in this lesson a word which is divided at the end of a line? What mark shows that the word is continued on the next line?
   Note: When a word is divided at the end of a line the division should be made between syllables.
   Note: A *hyphen (-)* is used at the end of a line to connect the syllables of a divided word.
7. Tell how the following words might be divided at the end of a line: *dreadful, imitated, excited.*

LESSON 26

LETTER WRITING

HELEN KELLER TO OLIVER WENDELL HOLMES

South Boston, MA
March 1, 1890

DEAR KIND POET:

I have thought of you many times since that bright Sunday when I bade you good-bye; and I am going to write you a letter because I love you. I am sorry that you have no little children to play with you sometimes; but I think you are very happy with your books, and your many, many friends.

On Washington's Birthday a great many people came here to see the blind children; and I read for them from your poems, and showed them some beautiful shells which came from a little island near Palos.

I am reading a very sad story called "Little Jakey." Jakey was the sweetest little fellow you can imagine, but he was poor and blind. I used to think—when I was small and before I could read—that everybody was always happy, and at first it made me very sad to know about pain and great sorrow; but now I know that we could never learn to be brave and patient if there were only joy in the world.

I am studying about insects in zoology, and I have learned many things about butterflies. They do not make honey for us like the bees, but many of them are as beautiful as the flowers they light upon, and they always delight the hearts of little children. They live a gay life flitting from flower to flower, sipping the drops of honeydew, without a thought for the morrow. They are just like boys and girls when they forget books and studies, and run away to the woods and fields to gather wild flowers or to wade in the ponds for fragrant lilies, happy in the bright sunshine.

If my little sister comes to Boston next June, will you let me bring her to see you? She is a lovely baby and I am sure you will love her.

Now I must tell my gentle poet good-bye, for I have a letter to write home before I go to bed.

From your loving little friend,
HELEN A. KELLER

This letter is taken from *A Story of My Life*, by Helen Keller.

1. How old was she when she wrote this letter?
2. Compare the date with the date of her birth.
3. To what does she compare butterflies? How do you suppose she could gain any knowledge of such insects?
4. Mention the central thought of each paragraph of this letter.
5. Arrange the topics in the form of an outline.

LESSON 27

LETTER WRITING

1. Read again the letter in Lesson 26.
2. Where was the letter written? What punctuation mark is placed between the name of the city and that of the state?

Note: The part of the letter that tells where it was written and when it was written is *the heading*. The letter begins, "Dear kind Poet." This part of the letter is called *the salutation*.
The *body of the letter* follows the salutation. The letter closes with "From your loving little friend." This is called *the complimentary close*. The *signature* of the person writing the letter follows the complimentary close.

3. What mark of punctuation follows the salutation? The complimentary close? The signature?
4. Write these headings from dictation:

A. Boston, MA
   Jan. 6, 1914

B. Jacksonville, FL
   June 16, 1914

C. Columbia University
   New York, NY
   Mar. 13, 1914

D. 1104 South Wabash Ave.
   Chicago, IL
   May 1, 1914

LESSON 28

LETTER WRITING

1. Write one of the following letters:
   A. Your friend, Charles White, who lives in the country, has sent you a puppy by express. Write a letter telling how you received the box, what the puppy did when you opened the box, what you have named him, and how you expect to train the dog.

   Thank your friend for sending you such a fine present, and invite him to visit you.
   B. Your Uncle Frank has sent you a fine box of fruit.

   Write a letter telling when it arrived and how pleased you were to receive it.   Tell with whom you shared part of your gift.

   Say that your parents have agreed to let you visit your uncle next summer and that you are looking forward to your summer vacation with much pleasure.

   Tell any items of interest concerning your family that your uncle might like to know.

Note: Your letter should have *heading, salutation, body, complimentary close, and signature*.

LESSON 29

ADDRESSING AN ENVELOPE

Mr. George W. Mitchell
1620 St. Charles Avenue
New Orleans, LA   70112

Note: **The envelope should contain the name of the person to whom the letter is to be sent, the street and number if the person lives in a city, the name of the city or town, and the name of the state.**
1. Address envelopes to the following:
A. Mrs. A. D. Clark, 1234 Avalon St., Milwaukee, WI, 53202.
B. Mr. Franklin D. Blackburn, 2313 Tara Drive, Birmingham, AL, 35216.
C. Miss Helen Brady, 2014 Third Avenue, Minneapolis, MN, 55416.
2. Where should the postage stamp be placed?

LESSON 30

SELECTION TO BE MEMORIZED

What plant we in this apple tree?
Buds which the breath of summer days
Shall lengthen into leafy sprays;
Boughs where the thrush, with crimson breast,
Shall haunt, and sing, and hide her nest;
We plant, upon the sunny lea,
A shadow for the noontide hour,
A shelter from the summer shower,
When we plant the apple tree.

—WILLIAM CULLEN BRYANT

1. Memorize the selection.

LESSON 31

DICTATION

If you live in a large city, you may not know the apple tree. In winter it is a short, grayish tree, with a flat or rounded top. Its stout, thick branches are irregular and rigid.

In the spring it is a white tree. Its large clusters of white and pink flowers look like short-stemmed bouquets with a margin of leaves below.

In autumn it is a green tree filled with fruit of red and gold.

—FROM *Ten Common Trees*

1. What is the central thought of each of these paragraphs?
2. Write the paragraphs about the apple tree from dictation.

LESSON 32

CONVERSATION—FRUITS

1. Tell what you can about the following fruits:

A. grapes	E. oranges	I. lemons
B. peaches	F. apples	J. bananas
C. currants	G. strawberries	K. plums
D. blackberries	H. pears	L. cranberries

2. Write sentences answering the following questions, each sentence to contain a series of words:
A. Which of these fruits grow on trees?
B. Which grow on vines?
C. Which grow on bushes?
D. Which grow only where it is always warm?
E. Which have you seen growing?
F. Which fruits can be shipped long distances?

LESSON 33

DESCRIPTION—A FRUIT STORE

1. Write a description of a fruit store, using the following outline:

A. Location of store
B. Owner
C. Kinds of fruit in the store
D. Parts of the world from which the fruit came
E. Losses in the fruit business
2. Parts A and B of the outline may be combined in one sentence.
3. Part C should contain words in a series.
4. Into how many paragraphs should your description be divided?

LESSON 34

CORRECT USE OF WORDS

A. Set the fern on the table.

B. You may sit in this chair.

C. Sit in a good position when you write.

D. We set the flowers in the window.

E. I sat under the big tree.

1. In which of the above sentences is an object referred to as placed in a certain position?

   Note: The word *sit* means to take a seat.

   Note: When an object is placed in any position the word *set* may be used.

2. Write six sentences telling—

   A. Where you set the dishes

   B. Where you set the geraniums

   C. Who set the dishes on the table

   D. Where you like to sit

   E. Who sits near you at school

   F. Who sits nearest the teacher's desk

3. Copy the following sentences, filling the blanks with *set, sit, or sat:*

   A. Mary, _____ the basket on the porch.

   B. Bring your chair and _____ near me.

C. _____ your doll in the doll carriage.

D. The dog likes to _____ near the fire.

E. I _____ near the window yesterday.

F. Do not be afraid; I will _____ near you.

G. _____ that bottle of ink on the desk.

LESSON 35

SELECTION FOR STUDY

THE BAREFOOT BOY

Blessings on thee, little
  man,
Barefoot boy, with cheek
  of tan!
With thy turned-up
  pantaloons,
And thy merry whistled
  tunes;
With thy red lip, redder
  still
Kissed by strawberries on
  the hill;
With the sunshine on thy
  face,
Through thy torn brim's
  jaunty grace;
From my heart I give
  thee joy—

JOHN GREENLEAF WHITTIER

I was once a barefoot boy!
Let the million-dollared ride!
Barefoot, trudging at his side,
Thou hast more than he can buy
In the reach of ear and eye—
Outward sunshine, inward joy:
Blessings on thee, barefoot boy!
Oh, for boyhood's painless play,
Sleep that wakes in laughing day,
Health that mocks the doctor's rules,
Knowledge never learned of schools,
Of the wild bee's morning chase,
Of the wild flower's time and place,
Flight of fowl and habitude
Of the tenants of the wood;
How the tortoise bears his shell,
How the woodchuck digs his cell,
And the ground mole sinks his well;
How the robin feeds her young,
How the oriole's nest is hung;
Where the whitest lilies blow,
Where the freshest berries grow,
Where the ground nut trails its vine,
Where the wood grape's clusters shine:
Of the black wasp's cunning way,
Mason of his walls of clay,
And the architectural plans
Of gray hornet artisans!

> For, eschewing books and tasks,
> Nature answers all he asks;
> Hand in hand with her he walks,
> Face to face with her he talks,
> Part and parcel of her joy—
> Blessings on the barefoot boy!
>
> —JOHN GREENLEAF WHITTIER

1. Consult the dictionary for meanings of the following words; divide the words into syllables and mark the accented syllables: *jaunty, habitude, architectural, artisans, eschewing.*
2. Describe the boy as the first stanza of the poem pictures him:
3. How was he dressed?
4. How old do you think he was?
5. If you were to draw a picture of him, what would you have him doing?
6. What background would you use?
7. Would the fifth and sixth lines suggest anything for your picture?
8. How did the poet know so much about a barefoot boy?
9. How does the barefoot boy have more than the rich man can buy?
10. Why is the wasp called a "mason"?
11. Tell what you can of an oriole's nest.

12. What knowledge does the boy have that he never learned in school?
13. Name some of the "tenants of the wood" that the boy might know.
14. Write the names of three insects, two birds, and three animals mentioned in the poem.
15. Write sentences telling something of the habits of each.
16. What flowers and fruits are mentioned?

LESSON 36

CONVERSATION—THE FARMER

1. Tell of the work of the farmer—

   A. in spring   C. in autumn
   B. in summer   D. in winter

2. What implements does the farmer use in his work?
3. How have modern inventions lightened the work of the farmer?
4. In what ways does the success of his work depend upon nature?
5. What kinds of crops are raised on farms in your section of the country?
6. Notice that the names of the seasons do not begin with capital letters.

LESSON 37

POSSESSIVE FORM

A. The barefoot boy knows how the oriole's nest is hung.

B. He knows the black wasp's cunning ways.

C. He has seen the woodchuck's cell.

1. Whose nest is mentioned in sentence A?

2. To what words are the *apostrophe* (') and *s* added to show ownership or possession?

   Note: Words written in this way to show ownership are said to be in the *possessive form*.

3. What words in sentences B and C are in the possessive form?

4. Find examples of the possessive form in Lessons 1, 3, 13, and 26.

5. Write sentences containing the following:

   A. the miller's boy   C. the barefoot boy's hat

   B. Pharaoh's daughter   D. the rich man's house

6. Use in sentences the possessive form of each of the following words:

   A. man   C. bluebird   E. angel

   B. king   D. squirrel   F. sister

LESSON 38

COMPOSITION

One morning in spring, Farmer Davis said, "I see that old Speckle wants to raise some more chickens. I think I will let her raise some ducks instead. I will get some ducks' eggs when I go to town this afternoon."

1. Copy the paragraph and complete the story by telling how long Speckle had to wait for the eggs to hatch, how the ducklings differed from little chickens, how Speckle took care of them, and what happened one day at the pond.

   Let the sentences in each paragraph of your story be about one central thought.

LESSON 39

NAMES

John Greenleaf Whittier wrote beautiful poems.
Note: Whittier is the *family name* or *surname*.
Note: John is the name that was given to the poet by his parents, and is called the *given name*.
Note: The name between the given name and the surname is the *middle name*.

1. With what kind of letter does each word of the name of a person begin?

Note: The first letter of a word is called an *initial.* **Mr. Whittier's initials are J. G. W.**

2. What punctuation mark is placed after an initial when used alone?

3. Write these names, using initials only for the given and middle names:

A. Oliver Wendell Holmes

B. James Russell Lowell

C. Ralph Waldo Emerson

D. William Cullen Bryant

LESSON 40

SELECTION FOR STUDY

STORY OF THE FLAX

The flax plant was in bloom; its little blue flowers were as delicate as the wings of a butterfly. The sun shone on it, the rain clouds gave it water, and the soft south wind blew it gently to and fro.

One day the farmer and his men came into the field. They took hold of the flax plant and pulled it up by the roots. Then they laid it in water, as if they were going to drown it, and after that they put it near a hot fire until it was almost burned up.

Then they broke it, they hackled it, and they combed it, until there was nothing left but the fine fibers of which its bark was made. A spinning wheel spun the fibers into long threads, and a loom wove the threads into a piece of beautiful white linen.

A mother bought the linen and made it into a dainty dress for her baby. But dresses wear out, and after a time this one was thrown into an ash barrel.

One day a rag picker found the linen rags and took them to a great mill. There they were soaked in hot water. They were ground into pulp and then passed under heavy rollers. Instead of linen rags, sheets of fine linen paper came out.

A bookmaker visited the mill. He bought the fine paper, and upon it were printed, soon after, the words of a great poet.

1. Make a list of the changes through which the flax passed.
2. Tell the story of the flax.
3. Into how many paragraphs is this story divided?
4. What is the central thought in each paragraph?
5. Tell what you can of looms and methods of weaving.
6. Tell something about the process of printing.
7. Write the first and second paragraphs from dictation.

LESSON 41

COMPOSITION—DESCRIPTION

1. Write a paragraph describing this book. Tell about—

    A. The cover—material, color, design
    B. The paper—thick or thin
    C. The print—large or small
    D. The margins—narrow or wide
    E. The illustrations

LESSON 42

COMPOSITION—THE THIRSTY CROW

A crow had had no water to drink for a long time. Seeing a pitcher she flew to it with great eagerness, but she found the water so low that she could not reach it. She tried to break the pitcher with her beak and then to overturn it with her foot, but her efforts were all in vain.

At last she thought of a plan: She picked up a number of little stones and dropped them one by one into the pitcher.

They fell to the bottom, and the water was soon raised so high that the thirsty crow was able to quench her thirst.

THE CROW'S STORY

I am so thirsty! I have had no water to drink for a long time. If I do not find some water soon, I shall die.

There is a pitcher, perhaps _____.

1. Copy these sentences, and complete the story as the crow might have told it.
Write your story in paragraphs.

LESSON 43

COMPOSITION—DIALOGUE

A grasshopper that loved to sing and dance met an ant that was putting away food for winter.

1. Write a conversation which may have taken place between the two, when the grasshopper urged the ant to play with him.
Use this form:
Grasshopper: Good morning, _____ _____.
Ant: _____ _____.
When winter came the grasshopper went to the ant's house begging for food.

2. Write the second conversation.

LESSON 44

CONVERSATION—THE CAT FAMILY

1. Talk about the house cat, from the following outline:

    A. Size
    B. Color
    C. Covering of body
    D. Feet—claws and soft pads
    E. Eyes
    F. Use of whiskers
    G. Roughness of tongue
    H. Teeth
    I. Food
    J. Method of hunting
    K. Habits
    L. Varieties of cats
    M. Use
    N. Cleanliness
    O. Friendliness
    P. Affection for young
    Q. Means of protection

Note: Animals that are similar in general structure and habits are said to belong to the same family.

2. The following animals belong to the cat family;

compare those you have seen with the house cat, using the points given in the outline:

A. lion   E. tiger
B. panther   F. wild cat
C. leopard   G. jaguar
D. puma   H. lynx

3. Write ten questions about an animal of the cat family. Read your questions, and call upon other pupils to answer.

4. Find and bring to class pictures of any of the animals mentioned in this lesson.

LESSON 45

COMPOSITION—DESCRIPTION OF AN ANIMAL

1. Write a description of one of the following animals:

A. tiger   F. dog
B. bear   G. wolf
C. cat   H. fox
D. rabbit   I. giraffe
E. squirrel   J. elephant

(Model your description after the one given in Lesson 44.)

LESSON 46

DICTATION—DESCRIPTION OF A LION

The lion is often called "the king of beasts." In height he varies from three to four feet, and he is from six to nine feet long. His coat is yellowish brown or tawny in color, and his neck is covered with a shaggy mane which gives his head a majestic appearance.

The home of the lion is in the forests of Asia or in Africa, where he is a terror to man and beast. He usually remains concealed during the day, but as the darkness comes on he prowls about where other animals are accustomed to go for food or drink. Hidden by the rocks or bushes, he waits until some creature comes near, then with a loud roar he springs upon his prey.

1. Use in sentences: A. height B. tawny C. shaggy D. terror E. prowls F. creature G. concealed
2. Why is the lion called "the king of beasts"?
3. Tell any stories of lions that you may have heard or read.
4. Make an outline of the description.
5. Write the description from dictation.

LESSON 47

REPRODUCTION—A FABLE

Two cats once found a piece of cheese, and they began to quarrel about it. Both cats claimed the cheese. One cat said that she had seen it first; the other said that she had picked it up first.

As they could not agree which should have the cheese, they called in a monkey and asked him to settle the quarrel.

The monkey said he would cut the cheese into two parts, and each cat could have one part. The cats thought this a fair arrangement, so the monkey cut the cheese with a knife.

He looked at the pieces and said he thought that one was a little larger than the other, so he took a bite off one piece. Then he said the other was larger, so he took a bite from that one.

The cats begged him to stop, but the monkey refused to give them the cheese until both parts had been made even. He nibbled first from one piece and then from the other.

At last he said that what was left was just enough to pay him for settling the quarrel. He quickly ate all that remained and ran away.

1. Write this fable in dialogue form.
Begin it in this way:

First Cat: This is my piece of cheese.

Second Cat: No, it is not yours. I saw it first.

First Cat: _____ _____ _____.

Second Cat: _____ _____ _____.

First Cat: _____ _____ _____.

Monkey: _____ _____ _____.

2. What punctuation mark is placed after the word *no*?

Note: The words *yes* and *no*, when used in answering questions, are generally followed by commas, except at the end of a sentence.

3. Find examples of the use of *yes* and *no*, in your readers.

LESSON 48

COMPOSITION

1. Read once more the story of "The Quarrel," Lesson 47.
2. Write a similar story about two little girls, a larger boy, and a ripe peach.
3. Where did the little girls get the ripe peach?
4. Why did they quarrel about it?
5. Whom did they ask to settle the quarrel?
6. What did the larger boy say?
7. What did he do?

LESSON 49

REPRODUCTION—A FABLE

1. Write in your own words one of the following fables:

    A. *The Fox in the Well*
    B. *The Hare and the Tortoise*
    C. *The Dog and His Shadow*
    D. *The Fox Who Lost His Tail*
    E. *The Wind and the Sun*
    F. *The Lion and the Mouse*
    G. *The Fox and the Crane*

    If you do not know any of these, write some other fable.

LESSON 50

IMAGINATIVE LETTER

1. A boy or girl has gone away for a visit, leaving a kitten at home. Write a letter from the kitten, which tells how it is being treated, what the other children in the house are doing, and how it wishes for the return of its master or mistress.

    Include some incident that might happen in the life of a kitten.

LESSON 51

SUMMARY

TO REMEMBER

The first word of every sentence begins with a capital letter.

The word *I* is written as a capital letter.

The first word of every line of poetry begins with a capital letter.

Names of persons and places begin with capital letters.

A title, when written with the name of a person, begins with a capital letter.

The names of the days of the week and the months of the year begin with capital letters.

The first word and each important word in titles of poems, books, etc., begin with capital letters.

A period is placed after a statement.

A period is placed after an abbreviation.

A period is placed after an initial when used alone.

A question mark is placed after a question.

Words of a series are separated by commas unless all the connecting words are expressed.

The words *yes* and *no*, when used in answering questions, are generally followed by commas except at the end of a sentence.

A hyphen is used at the end of a line to connect the syllables of a divided word.

A group of words that states something, or asks something, or expresses a command is called a sentence.

A paragraph is composed of one or more sentences about the same central thought.

A sentence that tells something is a statement.

A sentence that asks something is a question.

The parts into which a poem is divided are called stanzas.

LESSON 52

DICTATION—QUOTATION MARKS

A little red hen found a grain of wheat.
She said, "Who will plant this wheat?"
The rat said, "Not I."
The cat said, "Not I."
The pig said, "Not I."
"I will," said the little red hen, and she did.

1. Read what the hen said.

   Note: The marks that enclose the exact words spoken by the hen are called quotation marks (" ").
2. Where do you find other quotation marks?
3. Write the sentences from dictation.

LESSON 53

MEANING OF WORDS

1. Write a word opposite in meaning to each word of the following list; write the words in pairs, thus, *busy—idle:*

A.	honest	J.	large
B.	certain	K.	bitter
C.	broad	L.	sour
D.	deep	M.	industrious
E.	high	N.	generous
F.	heavy	O.	quiet
G.	wide	P.	tame
H.	valuable	Q.	slow
I.	rare	R.	difficult

2. Write other words that are opposite in meaning.
3. Write five sentences containing words and their opposites.

LESSON 54

SELECTION FOR STUDY

Don't Give Up

If you've tried and have not won,
  Never stop for crying;
All that's great and good is done
  Just by patient trying.

Though young birds, in flying, fall,
  Still their wings grow stronger;
And the next time they can keep
  Up a little longer.

Though the sturdy oak has known
  Many a blast that bowed her,
She has risen again, and grown
  Loftier and prouder.

If by easy work you beat,
  Who the more will prize you?
Gaining victory from defeat,
  That's the test that tries you!

—Phoebe Cary

1. What does this poem teach?
2. Explain "patient trying." What lessons in school require "patient trying?"

3. How may victory be gained from defeat? What may be learned from defeat?
4. If a football team is defeated, what may the players learn that will help when they play again?
5. If a pupil fails an examination, what may he learn from his failure?
6. Write the first and second stanzas of the poem from dictation.
7. Memorize the poem.

LESSON 55

CONTRACTIONS

1. What does *you've* mean, Lesson 54?
2. Write the two words for which *you've* stands.
3 What letters have been omitted?
Note: The mark showing that a letter or letters have been omitted is called an *apostrophe*.
Note: *You've* is a *contraction*.
4. Find another contraction in Lesson 54. For what words does it stand?
5. Write the words for which the following contractions stand: *I'm, can't, don't, I'll, they'll, we'll, you've, he's, it's, they're, couldn't, wouldn't.*
6. Write sentences containing five of these contractions.

LESSON 56

QUOTATIONS

A. The teacher said, "Someone is at the door."
B. Tom said, "It is not I."
C. "Perhaps it is Frank," said the teacher.
D. "I am sure it is not he," said Tom.
E. "Is it Lucile?" asked the teacher.
F. "It is not she," Tom replied.
G. "Then it must be Henry and Frank," said the teacher.
H. "Yes, it is they," said Tom.

1. Read the teacher's exact words, as used in sentence A.

   Note: These words are called a *direct quotation*.

2. Read the direct quotation given in sentence B.
3. What marks enclose the direct quotation?
4 What punctuation mark separates the direct quotation from the rest of the sentence?
5. With what kind of letter does the first word of a direct quotation begin?
6. Notice the use of *I, he, she,* and *they* in the sentences.

LESSON 57

DICTATION

1. Copy from Lesson 56 the conversation between the teacher and Tom. Pay special attention to punctuation.
2. Write the conversation from dictation.

LESSON 58

CORRECT USE OF WORDS

1. Write questions which might be answered by the following:
   A. It was I.
   B. It was not I; it was he.
   C. I think it was she.
   D. I am sure it is he.
   E. It was we.
   F. It might have been they.
   G. It is I.
   H. It was he and I.
   I. It was they.
   J. No, it is not he.
   K. Yes, it is she.
2. Write the answer after each of your questions.

LESSON 59

DESCRIPTION OF A GAME

Select one of the following exercises:

1. A. Draw a diagram of a baseball ground.
   B. Write a description of the game, telling how many players there are on a side, where the different players stand, and what points count in winning.
   C. Write three or more rules for the game.
2. A. Draw a diagram of a tennis court.
   B. Write a description of the game.
   C. Write two or more rules for the game.
3. A. Draw a diagram of a croquet ground.
   B. Write a description of the game.
   C. Write two or more rules for the game.
4. Write a description of the game you like best to play.

LESSON 60

LETTER WRITING

1. Your Aunt Ellen has sent you a ball and bat, a tennis racquet, or a croquet set, for a birthday present.

Write a letter thanking her: Say how kind you think she was to remember your birthday, tell where you play your games, and include any family news that you think might be of special interest to her.

REVIEW

2. Why does *Aunt* begin with a capital letter?
3. Name other words that begin with capital letters when used as parts of names.

LESSON 61

PICTURE STUDY—GAMBOLS OF CHILDREN

1. Tell what you see in the picture.
2. What is the meaning of the word "gambols?"
3. Can you suggest another name for the picture?
4. Are these American children? Give a reason for your answer.
5. Describe the background of the picture.
6. Tell a story that the picture suggests to you.
7. Which child do you think is the oldest?
8. Which is the youngest?
9. What do you think the man is telling the child on his lap?
10. What in the picture suggests happiness?

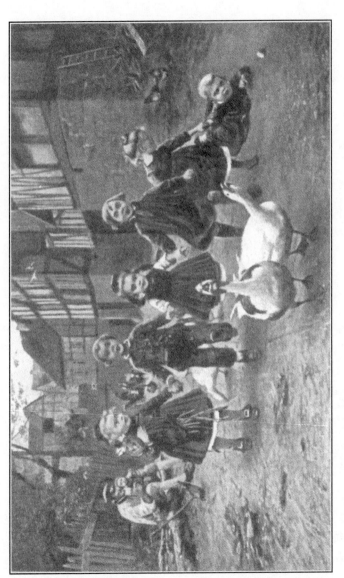

From a painting by Lins

GAMBOLS OF CHILDREN

LESSON 62

CORRECT USE OF WORDS

A. Birds *sing* in the leafy trees.

B. The artist *draws* pictures of strange scenes.

C. The bells *ring* loud and clear.

D. The rain *comes* to the thirsty flowers.

E. We *see* ripe apples in the orchard.

F. The farmer boy *drives* the cows to pasture.

G. The author *writes* a beautiful poem.

H. The cows *go* down to the river to drink.

I. The snow *falls* on the frozen ground.

J. The squirrel *eats* the sweet acorns from the oak trees.

1. Use one of the following groups of words in each of the above sentences, and change the italicized word in each sentence to show past time:

A. a few days ago	G. last September
B. last summer	H. two weeks ago
C. yesterday	I. a month ago
D. last week	J. last Christmas
E. day before yesterday	K. a long time ago
F. a year ago	L. last fall

2. Write sentences A-J, with one of the following groups of words in each; change the form of the

italicized word if necessary, and use with it the word
will; in sentence E use *shall* instead of *will*:

A. next week	F. next year
B. tomorrow	G. in a month
C. soon	H. next Christmas
D. in a few days	I. next September
E. next summer	J. next winter

3. Which sentences refer to present time?
4. Which sentences refer to past time?
5. Which sentences refer to future time?
6. Write the sentences again, using in each the word
has or *have*, and making necessary changes in
the italicized words.

LESSON 63

THE COMMA IN ADDRESS

A. "Mr. Brown, may we play baseball in your
vacant lot?"
B. "Yes, Harry, you may, if you will not be too
noisy."
C. "May I play, after school, Mother?"
1. Who is addressed in sentence A? What punctuation
mark is placed after the name?
2. Who is addressed in sentence B? What punctuation
marks are placed before and after the name?

3. Who is addressed in sentence C? What mark is placed before the name?

Note: The name of the person addressed is set off by a comma or commas.

4. Write sentences in which the following are addressed: *Mr. Davis, Cousin Clara, Grandfather, Rover, Dr. Andrews, Miss Taylor, Mother, Alfred, Baby.*

LESSON 64

ORAL COMPOSITION—A STORY

1. Complete a story from one of the following suggestions; tell your story to the class, from an outline that you have made:

A. One day Frank met an old lady who was carrying a heavy basket. He _____.

B. Nellie could not learn her spelling lesson. The words were not difficult, but _____.

C. One morning, when James came downstairs, he found the kitchen full of smoke. He _____.

D. Helen received a camera for a birthday present. She went _____.

E. Near the foot of a high hill was a thick undergrowth of brush, and here a mother rabbit had made her home. Every evening _____.

LESSON 65

SELECTION FOR STUDY

The Village Blacksmith

Under a spreading chestnut tree
The village smithy stands;
The smith, a mighty man is he,
With large and sinewy hands;
And the muscles of his brawny arms
Are strong as iron bands.

His hair is crisp, and black, and long,
His face is like the tan;
His brow is wet with honest sweat,
He earns whate'er he can,
And looks the whole world in the face,
For he owes not any man.

Week in, week out, from morn till night,
You can hear his bellows blow;
You can hear him swing his heavy sledge,
With measured beat and slow,
Like a sexton ringing the village bell,
When the evening sun is low.

And children coming home from school
Look in at the open door;

They love to see the flaming forge,
  And hear the bellows roar,
And catch the burning sparks that fly
  Like chaff from a threshing-floor.

He goes on Sunday to the church,
  And sits among his boys;
He hears the parson pray and preach,
  He hears his daughter's voice,
Singing in the village choir,
  And it makes his heart rejoice.

It sounds to him like her mother's voice,
  Singing in Paradise!
He needs must think of her once more,
  How in the grave she lies;
And with his hard, rough hand he wipes
  A tear out of his eyes.

Toiling—rejoicing—sorrowing,
  Onward through life he goes;
Each morning sees some task begun,
  Each evening sees it close;
Something attempted, something done,
  Has earned a night's repose.

Thanks, thanks to thee, my worthy friend,
  For the lesson thou hast taught!

Thus at the flaming forge of life
Our fortunes must be wrought;
Thus on its sounding anvil shaped
Each burning deed and thought.

—HENRY WADSWORTH LONGFELLOW

1. Describe the smith.
2. Where was the blacksmith shop?
3. What do you understand by the fifth and sixth lines of the second stanza?
4. To what is the beat of the sledge compared, in the third stanza?
5. Describe the picture in the fourth stanza.
6. Tell what you can of a blacksmith shop.
7. Explain:
   A. anvil B. forge C. bellows D. sledge
8. Describe the picture in the fifth stanza.
9. Tell what you think the last stanza means.
10. What is the lesson that has been taught?
11. Use in sentences the following: "spreading chestnut tree," "sinewy hands," "evening sun," "flaming forge," "a night's repose."
12. Who wrote this poem?
13. Can you tell the name of anything else this poet has written?

LESSON 66

HENRY WADSWORTH LONGFELLOW

HENRY W. LONGFELLOW

Picture to yourself a cozy library study in an old New England house, and in the room a man writing at the table. A white-haired man he is, with bright blue eyes and a mouth whose kindly smile cannot be hidden by the thick white beard. The man is Henry Wadsworth Longfellow, the best loved poet of America.

Mr. Longfellow lived in Cambridge, and many of his poems were written about something located near his home.

There was a chestnut tree that grew by a smithy. The poet often stopped in the shade of the tree to watch the brawny smith at his work, for, like the children in the poem, he loved to see the flaming forge and the burning sparks.

One day it was decided that the narrow street must be widened—and widening it meant cutting down the chestnut tree. Mr. Longfellow protested, but he could not save the great tree.

It was cut down, and then someone suggested that a chair be made of its wood, and be presented to the poet. The school children of the city brought their pennies and nickels to pay for the making of the chair, and one day it was sent to the home of their beloved friend.

1. Tell the story of the chestnut tree.

LESSON 67

SINGULAR AND PLURAL FORMS

Mr. Longfellow lived in Cambridge, and many of his poems were written about something located near his home.

1. In this sentence does the word *home* mean one home or more than one?
2. Does the word *poems* mean one poem or more than one?
   Note: When a word means one, it is said to be in the *singular* number.
   Note: When a word means more than one, it is said to be in the *plural* number.

3. Write the plurals of the following words:

A. poem	E. house	I. room
B. table	F. eye	J. smile
C. poet	G. tree	K. spark
D. street	H. chair	L. nickel

4. How is the plural of most words formed?

5. Copy twenty words in the singular number, from Lesson 66.

6. Copy five words in the plural number, from Lesson 65.

7. Write the singular of each of the following words:

A. churches	I. crosses
B. porches	J. glasses
C. birches	K. sashes
D. benches	L. taxes
E. arches	M. foxes
F. ditches	N. boxes
G. brushes	O. potatoes
H. lashes	P. echoes

8. How was the plural of the words you have written formed?

9. Notice the last two letters of each word included in the list.

LESSON 68

SELECTION FOR STUDY

THE WIND AND THE MOON

Said the Wind to the Moon, "I will blow you out;
      You stare
      In the air
      Like a ghost in a chair,
Always looking what I am about—
I hate to be watched; I'll blow you out."

The Wind blew hard, and out went the Moon.
      So, deep
      On a heap
      Of clouds to sleep,
Down lay the Wind, and slumbered soon,
Muttering low, "I've done for that Moon."

He turned in his bed; she was there again!
      On high
      In the sky,
      With her one ghost eye,
The Moon shone white and alive and plain.
Said the Wind, "I will blow you out again."
   *   *   *   *   *
He blew and he blew, and she thinned to a thread.
      "One puff
      More's enough
      To blow her to snuff!

One good puff more where the last was bred,
And glimmer, glimmer, glum will go the thread."

He blew a great blast, and the thread was gone.
          In the air
          Nowhere
          Was a moonbeam bare;
Far off and harmless the shy stars shone—
Sure and certain the Moon was gone!

The Wind he took to his revels once more;
          On down,
          In town,
          Like a merry-mad clown,
He leaped and helloed with whistle and roar—
"What's that?" The glimmering thread once more!

    *   *   *   *   *
Slowly she grew—till she filled the night,
          And shone
          On her throne
          In the sky alone,
A matchless, wonderful silvery light,
Radiant and lovely, the queen of the night.

Said the Wind: "What a marvel of power am I!
          With my breath,
          Good faith!
          I blew her to death—
First blew her away right out of the sky—
Then blew her in; what strength have I!"

But the Moon she knew nothing about the affair;
>   For high
>   In the sky,
>   With her one white eye,
Motionless, miles above the air,
She had never heard the great Wind blare.

—GEORGE MACDONALD

1. Why did the wind wish to blow out the moon?
2. In the second stanza, what happened to the moon? Then what did the wind do?
3. In the third stanza, what did the wind see when he "turned in his bed?"
4. In the fifth stanza, what is meant by the "thread?"
5. What happened when the wind "blew a great blast?"
6. Tell the story in the last three stanzas.
7. Describe the sky as it appeared in the first, second, fifth, sixth, seventh, and ninth stanzas.
8. In the first stanza, "stare," "air," and "chair" are said to "rhyme."
9. In the second stanza what words rhyme with the word "deep?"
10. Find words that rhyme in the other stanzas.
11. Use in sentences: A. slumbered B. ghost C. blast D. revels E. clown F. glimmering G. motionless H. silvery light I. affair

A COTTON FIELD

LESSON 69

CONVERSATION—CLOTHING

1. Mention different materials that are used for clothing.
Of what materials are the following made?

A. shoes	D. buttons	G. gingham	J. ribbon
B. hats	E. gloves	H. overcoats	K. mittens
C. socks	F. collars	I. raincoats	L. overshoes

2. Tell how these materials are obtained, and through what changes they pass in the process of manufacture.

LESSON 70

CONVERSATION—COTTON

A. Growing the cotton   E. Shipping by boat or train
B. Picking   F. At the mill
C. Ginning   G. Spinning into thread
D. Baling   H. Weaving into cloth

1. Tell all you can about cotton; group your sentences in paragraphs.

A COTTON GIN

LESSON 71

COMPOSITION—COTTON

1. Read again "The Story of the Flax," Lesson 40.
2. Using the outline given in Lesson 70, write the story of cotton.
3. Tell what happened to a single cotton plant.
4. After the weaving into cloth tell of the transportation to a store in your city or town.
5. Tell the story of the cloth.
6. Who bought the cloth?

LESSON 72

LETTER WRITING

1. Imagine that you are visiting a cousin on a cotton plantation in the South.
2. Write a letter home, telling of your arrival and your meeting with your cousin.
3. Write about your cousin's home and surroundings, his pets, and the good times you are having there.
4. Ask some questions about your own home, and send messages to members of your family and your friends.

LESSON 73

WORDS THAT RHYME

1. Write lists of words that rhyme with the following: *grow, kind, ground, talk, part, each, tree, brown, sun, ride, hear, nest, high, grand.*
2. Read the poem, "The Barefoot Boy," Lesson 35. Notice that the first line rhymes with the second. With what line does the third rhyme?
3. Write a stanza of four lines, making the first line rhyme with the second, and the third with the fourth.
4. Let your stanza be about one of the following: *a windy day, an oak tree, Christmas, football, a squirrel, a kitten, a bird, your schoolhouse.*
5. Write another stanza on any subject you wish.

LESSON 74

WRITING SENTENCES

Many hundred years ago, a Hebrew mother placed her baby boy in a tiny boat and hid him among the reeds by the river side.

1. In this sentence—
   A. Read the words that tell *when.*
   B. Read the words that tell *who.*

2. Read the words that tell two things that the mother did.

3. Write groups of words that tell *when*; as, *last fall.*

4. Use some of these groups of words in writing sentences similar in form to the first sentence in this lesson. Let your sentences be about—

A. an Indian boy   E. a rich man
B. a gray squirrel   F. George Washington
C. the king's daughter   G. an apple tree
D. an angel

LESSON 75

WRITTEN CONVERSATION

Nellie Taylor has moved into the house next to that of Bessie Brown. The two little girls are talking together.

1. Write the conversation—Nellie asking questions about the school and neighborhood, which Bessie answers.

Use the following form:
Bessie: I am so glad you are going to live near me. Are you going to school Monday?
Nellie: _____ _____ _____.

LESSON 76

LETTER WRITING

A boy has failed to pass an examination and wishes to leave school.

1. Write a letter urging him to try again.
2. Tell him of his need of an education, and offer to help him in making up the required work.

LESSON 77

POSSESSIVE FORM

A. Butter is made from the milk of cows.
B. Butter is made from cows' milk.
C. The eggs of hens are good to eat.
D. Hens' eggs are good to eat.
E. The bees' cells are filled with honey.

1. Read sentence A. Is the word *cows* singular or plural?
2. In sentence B, how is possession shown?
3. In sentence C, is the word *hens* singular or plural?
4. In sentence D, how is possession shown?
5. In sentence E, how is possession shown?

6. The following words are in the *possessive singular;* change them to *possessive plural:*

A. lion's
B. ant's
C. teacher's
D. pupil's
E. artist's
F. oak's
G. wren's
H. cricket's
I. merchant's
J. mother's

7. Use in sentences:

A. all the birds' nests
B. the bees' honey
C. boys' voices
D. squirrels' teeth
E. cats' feet
F. farmers' barns
G. dogs' collars
H. rabbits' ears
I. butterflies' wings
J. crickets' chirp

8. Change the following to sentences containing possessive forms:

A. The child listened for the music of the birds.
B. The blossoms of the apple trees are sweet.
C. The fierce roars of the lions frightened the other animals.
D. The soft light of the moonbeams fell across the floor.
E. The nest of the eagles was high up on the side of a mountain.
F. Claws of cats are curved and long.

LESSON 78

CONVERSATION—THE DOG FAMILY

1. Talk about the dog, using the following outline:
   A. Covering of body
   B. Feet
   C. Teeth
   D. Food
   E. Method of hunting
   F. Habits
   G. Keen sense of smell
   H. Varieties of dogs
   I. Use
   J. Friendliness
   K. Bravery
   L. Intelligence

2. When are animals said to *belong to the same family*? (See Lesson 44.)
3. The following animals belong to the dog family; compare those that you have seen with the dog, using the points given in the outline:
   A. wolf B. fox C. coyote D. hyena E. jackal
4. Write ten statements about an animal of the dog family.
5. Bring to class pictures of any of the animals mentioned in this lesson.

From a painting by J. G. Brown THE WOUNDED COMPANION

LESSON 79

PICTURE STUDY—THE WOUNDED COMPANION

1. Describe the picture.
2. To which boy do you think the dog belongs?
3. Tell the story suggested by the picture.
4. What is the artist's name?
5. Find another picture by the same artist, in this book.

LESSON 80

COMPOSITION—STORY ABOUT WOOL

Frank Wentworth lived many years ago when this great country of ours was new. Winter was coming, and Mother Wentworth knew that Frank would need a heavy coat to keep him warm when the north wind piled the great snowdrifts high around the door.

1. Copy the paragraph and complete the story, telling about—
   A. Cutting the wool from the sheep
   B. Combing or carding it into long rolls
   C. Spinning it into yarn on the spinning wheel
   D. Dyeing it in the big kettle

E. Weaving the yarn into cloth on the loom
F. Making the cloth into a coat

2. Let your story contain conversation between Frank and his mother, concerning the work.

LESSON 81

CORRECT USE OF WORDS

A. "May I help you, Mother?"
B. "You may help cut the wool, Frank, but I doubt if you can spin it."
C. "I am sure I can spin it; please, let me try."

1. Read the sentence that asks permission.
2. Read the part of sentence B that grants the desired permission.
3. Read the parts of sentences B and C that relate to Frank's ability to spin.
4. Notice the use of *can* and *may*.
5. Write six sentences containing the word *may*, in which you ask permission of your mother or teacher to do certain things.
6. Write ten sentences containing the word *can*, in which you ask different classmates concerning their ability to do certain things.

LESSON 82

COMPOSITION—FRISK AND THE MIRROR

One day Frisk saw himself in the mirror, which his mistress had been dusting.

He thought he saw another dog. What do you think happened?

1. Tell or write the story as if Frisk were telling it. Begin the story in this way:

This morning, when I went into the dining room, I was much surprised to see another dog standing in front of me.

SHEPHERD AND SHEEP

LESSON 83

PICTURE STUDY—SHEPHERD AND SHEEP

1. Describe the picture.
2. What time of year do you think it is? Give a reason for your answer.
3. What time of day do you think it is?
4. Which part of the picture interests you more, the sheep or the surroundings?
5. Does such a picture make you long to be in the woods?
6. What would you do if you had an afternoon to spend in such a place?
7. Of what use to a shepherd is a dog?
8. Tell any stories that you may have read about shepherd dogs.

LESSON 84

CORRECT USE OF WORDS

A. The shepherd *gives* food to the sheep.
B. He *knows* the best pasture.
C. The lambs *run* through the grass.
D. Wolves *steal* some of the lambs.
E. The shepherd *speaks* to his dog.
F. He *takes* a lamb in his arms.

1. Change the sentences so that they will refer to some time in the past.
2. Change the sentences so that they will refer to some time in the future.
3. Change the sentences, using in each the word *has* or *have.*

LESSON 85

SINGULAR AND PLURAL

Note: The plurals of some words are formed in irregular ways.

1. Learn the following:

SINGULAR	PLURAL
A. mouse	mice
B. ox	oxen
C. goose	geese
D. foot	feet
E. man	men
F. woman	women
G. tooth	teeth
H. child	children

Note: The following words have the same form for both singular and plural: *sheep, deer, moose.*

2. Copy, from Lesson 40, ten words that are plural; change them to the singular number.

LESSON 86

A LEGEND ABOUT KING SOLOMON

KING SOLOMON AND THE BEES

When Solomon was reigning in his glory,
    Unto his throne the queen of Sheba came—
So in the Talmud you may read the story—
    Drawn by the magic of the monarch's fame,
To see the splendors of his court, and bring
Some fitting tribute to the mighty king.

Nor this alone: much had her highness heard
    What flowers of learning graced the royal speech;
What gems of wisdom dropped with every word;
    What wholesome lessons he was wont to teach
In pleasing proverbs; and she wished, in sooth,
To know if rumor spoke the simple truth.

Besides, the queen had heard (which piqued her most)
    How through the deepest riddles he could spy;
How all the curious arts that women boast
    Were quite transparent to his piercing eye;
And so the queen had come—a royal guest—
To put the sage's cunning to the test.

And straight she held before the monarch's view,
    In either hand, a radiant wreath of flowers;
The one, bedecked with every charming hue,
    Was newly culled from nature's choicest bowers;
The other, no less fair in every part,
Was the rare product of divinest art.

"Which is the true and which the false?" she said.
Great Solomon was silent.   All amazed,
Each wondering courtier shook his puzzled head;
    While at the garlands long the monarch gazed,
As one who sees a miracle, and fain,
For very rapture, ne'er would speak again.

"Which is the true?" once more the woman asked,
    Pleased at the fond amazement of the king;
"So wise a head should not be hardly tasked,
    Most learned liege, with such a trivial thing!"
But still the sage was silent; it was plain
A deepening thought perplexed the royal brain.

While thus he pondered, presently he sees,
    Hard by the casement—so the story goes—
A little band of busy, bustling bees,
    Hunting for honey in a withered rose.
The monarch smiled and raised his royal head;
"Open the window!" that was all he said.

The window opened at the king's command;
    Within the room the eager insects flew,
And sought the flowers in Sheba's dexter hand!
    And so the king and all the courtiers knew
That wreath was nature's; and the baffled queen
Returned to tell the wonders she had seen.

—JOHN G. SAXE

1. Why did the Queen of Sheba travel far to see Solomon?
2. What had she heard with regard to the great Hebrew king?
3. How did she test his wisdom?
4. What was the result of the test?
5. Write the story of "King Solomon and the Bees," using the following words: *monarch, tribute, proverbs, rumor, piqued, transparent, radiant, culled, garlands, amazement, trivial, perplexed, withered, baffled.*
6. Arrange your story in paragraphs, and let it contain at least two direct quotations.

LESSON 87

COMPOSITION—A STORY

1. Tell the fable of "The Hare and the Tortoise."
2. Write a similar story about two boys: Frank, who learns everything easily, and Carl, who has to work hard to learn his lessons.

   A prize has been offered for the pupil who spells the most words correctly.

   Show how Carl won the prize.
3. Let your story contain some direct quotations.

LESSON 88

SELECTION FOR STUDY

DAYBREAK

A wind came up out of the sea,
And said, "O mists, make room for me!"

It hailed the ships, and cried, "Sail on,
Ye mariners, the night is gone!"

And hurried landward far away,
Crying, "Awake! It is the day!"

It said unto the forest, "Shout!
Hang all your leafy banners out!"

It touched the wood-bird's folded wing,
And said, "O bird, awake and sing!"

And o'er the farms, "O chanticleer,
Your clarion blow; the day is near!"

It whispered to the fields of corn,
"Bow down, and hear the coming morn!"

It shouted through the belfry tower,
"Awake, O bell! Proclaim the hour."

It crossed the churchyard with a sigh,
And said, "Not yet! In quiet lie."

—HENRY WADSWORTH LONGFELLOW

1. Give the meaning of "mariners," "chanticleer," "clarion," "belfry," "proclaim."
2. What effect does the wind have on the mists?
3. Who or what is meant by "it" in the second stanza?
4. What words might have been used in place of "landward" in the third stanza?
5. Explain "leafy banners" in the fourth stanza.
6. Explain the sixth stanza.
7. What do you understand by the last stanza?
8. Use in sentences: "hailed," "landward," "leafy banners," "fields of corn."
9. To what different things did the wind speak?
10. How many different quotations are there in the poem?
11. What contraction do you find?
12. Find examples of the person or thing addressed.
13. Who wrote the poem?

LESSON 89
DICTATION

1. Write from dictation the first four stanzas of "Daybreak," Lesson 88.

LESSON 90

EXCLAMATIONS

The wind said unto the forest, "Shout!"
It called to the ships, "Awake! The night is gone!"
The sailors shouted, "Hurrah! The day has come!"

1. Where are exclamation points (!) placed in these sentences?
2. How many exclamations can you find in the poem, Lesson 88?
3. Write exclamations which you might use—
    A. If you had lost some money
    B. If you had found it again
    C. If you had received a gift
    D. If you heard something that greatly surprised you
    E. If you were hurt
    F. If you wished someone to keep quiet
    G. If you had won a game
    H. If you had lost a game
    I. If you were in need of help
    J. If you were tired
    K. If you were given a holiday

LESSON 91

AN AUTOBIOGRAPHY

Note: An autobiography is an account of one's life written by himself.

1. Use the following outline in writing your autobiography:

A. Name
B. Birthplace
C. Date of birth
D. Residence
E. School life
F. Name of school
G. Name of teacher
H. Grade
I. Studies
J. Occupations outside of school
K. Favorite games or sports
L. Favorite books
M. Pets
N. Friends
O. Interesting or exciting events in your life
P. Plans for the future
Q. Education
R. Business

LESSON 92

STORY OF A MEADOWLARK

Once upon a time, a child sat under an oak tree near a stream of water. She seemed very sad, for now and then a tear rolled down her face and fell upon the grass.

Presently, where the tears had fallen, something moved. The child turned and beheld at her side a beautiful meadowlark.

1. Complete this story.
2. What was the meadowlark's first question?
3. What was the little girl's answer?
4. What did the meadowlark do to help the child?
5. Think of your story and make an outline that you can use in telling it.
6. What exclamations might the child use when she sees the meadowlark?
7. What exclamations might the meadowlark use when she hears the sad story of the little girl?
8. What exclamations might the child use to show her happiness, after the meadowlark had helped her?
9. Use in your story—
   A. Quotation marks
   B. Possessive form

LESSON 93

COMPOSITION—TWO SQUIRRELS

1. Write or tell a story about two little squirrels that lived in an old elm tree.

2. Include in your story some incident that might happen in the life of a squirrel.

3. What enemies has a squirrel?

4. What narrow escape might a squirrel have?

LESSON 94

CONVERSATION—GNAWERS OR RODENTS

1. Talk about the squirrel, from the following outline:

A. Size

B. Covering of body

C. Color

D. Feet

E. Teeth

F. Food

G. Provision for winter

H. Habits

2. Why is a squirrel called a gnawer?

3. When are animals said to belong to the same family?

4. Tell what you can of the—
   A. beaver   E. chipmunk   I. prairie dog
   B. rabbit   F. porcupine   J. woodchuck
   C. mouse   G. guinea pig
   D. hare   H. rat

LESSON 95

CORRECT USE OF WORDS

A. Tom and Henry are both tall, but I believe Henry is the taller.
B. There are several tall boys in the class, but Frank is the tallest.

1. In sentence A how many boys are compared?
2. What is added to *tall* to indicate the comparison?
3. In sentence B, where more than two are compared, what is added to *tall?*

Note: When words are long they are usually compared by prefixing *more* and *most*; as, beautiful, *more* beautiful, *most* beautiful. Note: Some words are compared irregularly; as, *good, better, best.*

1. Fill the blanks in the following sentences with words chosen from the list on page 100:
   A. I have only a little money and she has _____.
   B. Which is the _____ of the two boys?
   C. There are many pretty pictures in the room; which do you think is the _____?

D. This is a _____ apple, but that one is
_____.

E. You took the _____ apple in the basket.

F. Sugar is _____, but honey is _____.

G. This is an amusing story, but that one is
_____.

H. Today is cold, Saturday was _____, and last
Friday was the _____ day of this month.

I. Which of the two babies is the _____?

J. Which of the three babies is the _____?

K. This orchard has a great many trees, but
the orchard across the street has _____.

L. All the trees have apples on them, but this
one has _____.

M. Which tree in the orchard is _____ from
the road?

little	less	least
old	older	oldest
good	better	best
pretty	prettier	prettiest
large	larger	largest
sweet	sweeter	sweetest
cold	colder	coldest
amusing	more amusing	most amusing
young	younger	youngest
many	more	most
far	farther	farthest

LESSON 96

CONVERSATION—MONEY

1. Name different kinds of money.
2. Of what is a penny made?
3. Of what is a nickel made?
4. Name some money that is made of silver.
5. Of what is a quarter made?
6. Why is a quarter smaller than a silver dollar piece?
7. Why are the edges of some coins notched?
8. In what is the right to coin money vested?
9. What is the place where money is coined called?
10. Examine a piece of money.
11. Tell what printing and pictures you find.
12. Explain the meaning of the pictures.
13. Examine and describe a piece of paper money.

LESSON 97

COMPOSITION—HISTORY OF A DIME

One morning in winter, a shining dime came from the mint and began its journey in the world.

It went first to a bank, where _____.

1. Complete the story, telling of the different people who used the dime. Trace it until it is finally lost in a lake or river.

LESSON 98

PICTURE STUDY

RETURN OF THE FISHING BOATS

1. Look carefully at the picture, then close your eyes and try to see it.
2. Does the picture suggest any body of water that you have seen?
3. Have you seen sailboats? If you have, tell something about them.
4. What time of the day do you think it is?
5. Where have the boats been?
6. Can you think of a story suggested by the picture?
7. Suppose a boy twelve years old were on the boat, what story might he tell?
8. Do you think this picture could be used to illustrate any poem in this book?
9. What part of the poem suggests the picture?

RETURN OF THE FISHING BOATS

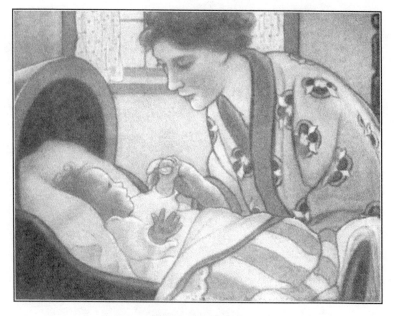

LESSON 99

SELECTION TO BE MEMORIZED

SWEET AND LOW

Sweet and low, sweet and low,
    Wind of the western sea;
Low, low, breathe and blow,
    Wind of the western sea!
Over the rolling waters go,
Come from the dying moon, and blow,
    Blow him again to me;
While my little one, while my pretty one, sleeps.

Sleep and rest, sleep and rest,
    Father will come to thee soon;
Rest, rest, on Mother's breast,
    Father will come to thee soon;
Father will come to his babe in the nest,
Silver sails all out of the west,
    Under the silver moon;
Sleep, my little one, sleep, my pretty one, sleep.

—ALFRED TENNYSON

1. Do you like the poem? Why?
2. Who is supposed to be saying or singing it?
3. What picture does the poem suggest?
4. What lines suggest that the father may be out on the sea?
5. What do you understand by "rolling waters?"
6. Name the words that describe "moon."
7. Explain "dying moon."
8. Which lines end in words that rhyme?
9. Which lines end in the same word?
10. Explain the marks of punctuation in the last line of the poem.
11. Who wrote this poem?
12. Memorize the poem.
13. Write the first stanza from memory.
14. Which words in the first stanza rhyme with "low?"
15. Which words in the second stanza rhyme with "rest?"

LESSON 100

SUMMARY—Continued from Lesson 51

TO REMEMBER

Direct quotations are enclosed in quotation marks.
The first word of a direct quotation begins with a capital letter.
A direct quotation is separated from the rest of the sentence by a comma.
The name of the person addressed is separated from the rest of the sentence by commas.
An exclamation point is always placed after an exclamation.
Words in the singular refer to one object.
Words in the plural refer to more than one object.
Most words form the plural by adding *s* to the singular.
Words in the singular form the possessive by adding the apostrophe and *s*.
Words in the plural, ending in *s*, form the possessive by adding the apostrophe.
An apostrophe is used in a contraction, to show that one or more letters have been omitted.

Part Two

LESSON 101

SELECTION FOR STUDY

The Story of a Seed

Long, long ago, two seeds lay beside each other in the earth, waiting. It was cold and rather wearisome, and, to pass away the time, the one found means to speak to the other.

"What are you going to be?" said the one.

"I don't know," answered the other.

"For me," replied the first, "I mean to be a rose. There is nothing like a splendid rose. Everybody will love me then."

"It's all right," whispered the second; and that was all it could say. For somehow when it had said that, it felt as if all the words in the world were used up. So they were silent again for a day or two.

"Oh, dear!" cried the first. "I have had some water. I never knew until it was inside me. I am growing! I'm growing! Good-bye."

"Good-bye," repeated the other, and lay still and waited more patiently than ever.

The first grew and grew, pushing itself straight up, till at last it felt that it was in the open air; for it could breathe. And what a delicious breath it was! It was rather cold, but so refreshing.

It could see nothing, for it was not quite a flower yet—only a plant. Plants never see until their eyes come—that is, till they open their blossoms; then, they are flowers indeed.

So it grew and grew, and kept its head up very steadily. It meant to see the sky the first thing, and leave the earth quite behind, as well as beneath it. But somehow or other—though why it could not tell—it felt very much inclined to cry.

At length it opened its eye. It was morning, and the sky was over its head. But, alas! It was no rose—only a tiny white flower.

It felt yet more inclined to hang down its head and cry. But it still resisted, and tried hard to open its eye, and to hold its head upright, and to look full at the sky.

"I will be a Star of Bethlehem, at least," said the flower to itself.

But its heart felt very heavy, and a cold wind rushed over it and bowed it down toward the earth. And the flower saw that the time of the singing of birds had not come, that the snow covered the whole land, and that there was not a single flower in sight but itself.

It half closed its leaves in terror and the dismay of loneliness. But that instant it remembered what the other seed used to say, and it said to itself, "It's all right; I will be what I can."

And then it yielded to the wind, drooped its head to the earth, and looked no more to the sky, but on the snow.

And straightway the wind stopped, the cold died away, and the snow sparkled like pearls and diamonds. The flower knew that it was the holding up of its head that hurt it so, and that its body came of snow, and that its name was Snowdrop.

And so it said once more, "It's all right," and waited in perfect peace; it needed only to hang its head after its nature.   —GEORGE MACDONALD

Note: Sometimes a direct quotation is divided by other words. As, "For me," replied the first, "I mean to be a rose."

1. Observe carefully the punctuation of the divided quotation.

2. In this lesson find exclamations, contractions, divided quotations.

3. Tell "The Story of a Seed."

4. Use in sentences: *wearisome, patiently, delicious, refreshing, inclined, dismay, yielded, straightway.*

LESSON 102

DICTATION

1. Write from dictation the first twelve lines of "The Story of a Seed," Lesson 101.

LESSON 103

DIVIDED QUOTATIONS

1. Change the following to divided quotations:
   A. The first replied, "I mean to be a rose. There is nothing like a splendid rose."
   B. "I'm growing! Good-bye," the seed replied.
   C. The seed said to itself, "It's all right; I will be what I can."
2. Write quotations, each of which shall be divided by one of the following expressions:
   A. replied the soldier
   B. shouted the north wind
   C. said the barefoot boy
   D. I answered
   E. laughed Harry
   F. the girl said
   G. called the captain
   H. said the little red hen
   I. he said to himself

LESSON 104

DIVIDED QUOTATIONS

One day, a crow who had found a piece of cheese started to take it home to her little ones. As she was resting in a tree, a fox passed by. He wished to have the cheese, so he began to talk to the crow. The crow did not reply.

The fox told her how beautiful she was, and how glossy her feathers were, but the crow made no answer.

At last he told her he had heard that her voice was very beautiful, but he could not be sure of it until he had heard her sing. He begged for one little song. The crow was so pleased with the words of the fox that she opened her mouth and gave a loud caw.

As she did so the cheese fell to the ground, and the fox quickly ate it up.

1. Write this story, changing as much of it as possible to direct quotations.
2. Let some of the quotations be divided by such expressions as, *said the fox, the fox begged*, etc.
3. Add other remarks that the fox might have made.
4. After each remark of the fox refer in some way to the crow.
5. Tell what the crow may have thought as she flew homeward.

LESSON 105

INDIRECT QUOTATIONS

A. The fox told the crow he had heard that her voice was very beautiful.

B. The fox said, "I have heard that your voice is very beautiful."

C. The fox begged for one little song.

D. "Won't you please sing one little song for me?" begged the fox.

1. Which of these sentences contain *direct quotations?*

2. Which do not contain the *exact* words of the speaker?

Note: Sentences A and C are called *indirect quotations*, because they give the thought of the speaker, but not his exact words.

3. Copy, from Lesson 88, a sentence containing a direct quotation; change it to an indirect quotation.

4. Copy, from Lesson 56, two sentences containing direct quotations; change them to indirect quotations.

5. Copy, from Lesson 101, four sentences containing direct quotations; change them to indirect quotations.

LESSON 106

COMPOSITION—A STORY

As Paul Carter was going on an errand one day, he found a pocketbook by the side of the walk.

1. Write the story, mentioning:
   A. The contents of the pocketbook
   B. What Paul was tempted to do
   C. What he decided to do
   D. How he returned the pocketbook to the owner

If possible, let your story contain indirect quotations and direct quotations; let one or more of the direct quotations be divided.

LESSON 107

CONVERSATION—THE BODY

1. What holds the body erect?
2. What moves the body?
3. What is the outer covering of the body called?
4. What organ pumps the blood through the body?
5. How does the blood reach all parts of the body?
6. Where are the lungs located?

7. How are the lungs and the heart protected?
8. Of what use are the lungs?
9. Of what advantage are joints?
10. Compare the elbow joint with the wrist joint. Which joint moves only backward and forward?
11. Compare the wrist joint with other joints of the body.
12. Of what use are fingernails?
13. Where is food digested?
14. What part of the eye has the power of sight?
15. In how many directions can you look without turning your head?
16. Of what use are eyebrows?
17. Of what use are eyelids?
18. Where is the voice produced?
19. Of what use is the tongue?
20. Where is the palate?
21. Describe the mouth.
22. Where is the brain located?
23. How is it protected?
24. Of what use are the nerves?
25. Name the five senses.
26. Which sense is the most important?

LESSON 108

DEBATE

The sense of sight is more important than the sense of hearing.

1. Let two pupils debate the question, one taking the affirmative side and the other the negative.

   Note: The speaker for the affirmative should tell of the benefits that sight gives, the work that could not be done except by means of the eyes, and the many pleasures it brings.

2. State arguments that may be presented by the negative side and answer them.

   Note: The speaker for the negative should tell of the benefits of hearing and its pleasures.

3. Reply to the arguments given by the speaker for the affirmative and show any mistakes he may have made in reasoning.

4. Let the class decide which pupil has presented the stronger argument.

5. The pupils who take part in the debate should make outlines of their speeches.

   Note: As a rule the strongest arguments should be placed last.

LESSON 109
LETTER WRITING—REVIEW

1. Write the heading that you would use if writing a letter from your home today.
2. Write the heading that you would have used for sending a letter from some city near your home last Christmas.
3. Write the heading that you might use for sending a letter from London on your next birthday.
4. Write the salutations that you would use in addressing your mother; your cousin; your uncle; your teacher; a classmate.
5. Write a complimentary close for each of these letters.
6. Write a note asking a classmate to go home from school with you. Tell about some pet, game, or new book that you would like to show.
8. Write an answer to the note, telling why you cannot go to his home today. Ask your friend if he would like to read the book you received for your birthday recently.

LESSON 110

HOMONYMS

Note: Words that are alike in sound but different in meaning are called *homonyms*.

1. Find the meaning of the following homonyms and use each in a sentence:

A. steal
   steel
B. knot
   not
C. feet
   feat
D. beet
   beat

E. ate
   eight
F. sun
   son
G. no
   know
H. hour
   our

I. would
   wood
J. lye
   lie
K. fore
   four
L. meet
   meat

2. Fill the blanks in the following sentences with words from the list above:

A. The bridge was ninety _____ long and was constructed of _____ and iron.
B. The athlete performed a dangerous_____.
C. We _____ sugar that was made from the sugar _____.
D. I will _____ you there in an _____.
E. Soap is made from _____ ashes and _____.
F. The hail _____ the blossoms from the fruit trees.

From a painting by Cope

DEPARTURE OF THE PILGRIMS FROM DELFT HAVEN

LESSON 111

PICTURE STUDY

Departure of the Pilgrims

1. Tell the story of the Pilgrims.
2. Why had they left their homes in England to go to Holland?
3. How were they treated in Holland?
4. Why did they wish to go to America?
5. Describe the picture.
6. Tell something of the occupants of the boat.
7. Do they seem glad or sorrowful?
8. Describe the people on the shore.
9. Tell anything you can concerning the voyage and the early days in America.

LESSON 112

CONVERSATION—FOODS

Note: A list of articles of food arranged in the order in which they are to be served at a meal is called a *menu*.

1. Write a menu for a Thanksgiving dinner.
2. Mention the source of each article of food.
3. Make a list of the countries that contributed to the dinner.

4. Tell about the transportation of articles.
5. Tell through what processes each article had to pass before it was ready to be eaten.
6. Mention some of the people who aided in its preparation.
7. Classify foods under these heads:
   A. animal B. vegetable C. mineral.

LESSON 113

COMPOSITION—A LOAF OF BREAD

1. Write the history of a loaf of bread.
2. Begin with the wheat that the farmer sowed. Use the following outline:

   A. Sowing the wheat
   B. The wheat field
   C. The rain
   D. The sunshine
   E. Cutting the wheat
   F. The threshing
   G. The mill
   H. The grinding
   I. The flour
   J. Transportation of the flour
   K. Sale of the flour in the store
   L. Making the bread

LESSON 114

THANKSGIVING

Praise God for wheat, so white and sweet, of which
  we make our bread!
Praise God for yellow corn, with which His waiting
  world is fed!
Praise God for fish and flesh and fowl, He gave to man
  for food!
Praise God for every creature which He made, and
  called it good!

Praise God for winter's store of ice! Praise God for
  summer's heat!
Praise God for fruit tree bearing seed; "to you it is
  for meat!"
Praise God for all the bounty by which the world is
  fed!
Praise God, His children all, to whom He gives their
  daily bread!
                              —EDWARD EVERETT HALE

1. Talk about the meaning of this poem.
2. Name the things mentioned in the poem, which
   God has given to man for food.
3. Mention other things that you have reason to
   be thankful for.

4. With what kind of letter does the word *God* begin?
5. Find in the poem other words referring to God.
6. With what kind of letters do these words begin?

LESSON 115

SINGULAR AND PLURAL

SINGULAR	PLURAL
A. wolf	E. wolves
B. shelf	F. shelves
C. wife	G. wives
D. calf	H. calves

1. Study the words. Which of the words end in the singular?
2. Which ends in *fe*?
3. In forming the plural, *f* or *fe* is changed to what letters?
4. Write the plural of the following:

A. knife	E. thief
B. life	F. beef
C. self	G. loaf
D. half	H. sheaf

5. Copy the following sentence, filling the blanks to make a rule for this formation of the plural:
6. Most words ending in *f* or *fe* form the plural by changing _____ or _____ to _____.

LESSON 116

CONVERSATION—CUD CHEWERS

1. Talk about the cow, using the following outline:
   A. Size
   B. Covering of body
   C. Feet
   D. Teeth
   E. Food
   F. Habits
   G. Use—milk, meat, hide, hair, etc.
   H. Means of protection

2. Why is the cow called a *cud chewer?*
3. Tell what you can of the following cud chewers, stating in what respects they are like the cow:

   A. goat   D. deer
   B. giraffe   E. sheep
   C. antelope   F. buffalo

4. Name some animals that belong to the *cat family.*
5. Name some animals that belong to the *dog family.*
6. Name some animals that are *rodents.*

From a painting by Landseer
THE DEER FAMILY

LESSON 117

PICTURE STUDY—THE DEER FAMILY

Edwin Landseer was born in the city of London in 1802. He was not more than five or six years old when he began to draw pictures of the animals he saw in the streets. His father was proud of the work of the little boy and often helped him to make the drawings better.

When the boy was older, he used to go to the Zoological Garden, and there he made pictures of bears, lions, and tigers.

The people of London began to buy the pictures that young Landseer offered for sale. With the money earned thus, he bought a home in the country, where he could keep dogs, deer, sheep, goats, and other animals that he wished to paint.

1. Describe the picture, *The Deer Family.*
2. Which is the father deer?
3. Tell what you can of the habits of deer.
4. What do they eat?
5. Where are they found?   Did you ever see one?
6. Read the first and second paragraphs in this lesson, and complete the following sentences:
7. "Landseer" begins with a capital letter, because ————.

8. There is a period after 1802 because _____.
9. *London* begins with a capital letter, because _____.
10. *When* begins with a capital letter, because _____.
11. There is a comma after *bears*, because _____.

LESSON 118

CORRECT USE OF WORDS

A. Sweet blossoms *grow* on the apple trees.
B. The sun *shines* upon them.
C. The birds *begin* to build a nest.
D. They *choose* a place in a tall tree.
E. They *bring* feathers to line the nest.
F. They *fly* to the garden for bugs.
G. The wind *blows* loud and shrill.
H. It *breaks* the branches from the tall tree.
I. It *shakes* the tree and the nest falls to the ground.

1. Change these sentences so that they will refer to some time in the past. Change the italicized words.
2. Rewrite the sentences so that they will refer to some time in the future. Change the italicized words if necessary.
3. Rewrite the sentences, using in each the word *has* or *have*. Change the italicized words.

LESSON 119

SELECTION FOR STUDY

THE WINDFLOWER

"Windflower, Windflower, why are you here?
This is a boisterous time of the year
For blossoms as fragile and tender as you
To be out on the roadsides, in spring raiment new.
The snowflakes yet flutter abroad on the air,
And the sleet and the tempest are weary to bear;
Have you not come here, pale darling, too soon?
You would seem more at home with the blossoms in June."

"Why have I come here?" the Windflower said;
"Why?" and she gracefully nodded her head
As a breeze touched her petals. "Perhaps to show you
That the strong may be sometimes the delicate, too.
I am fed and refreshed by these cold, rushing rains;
The first melting snowdrifts brought life to my veins;
The storm rocked my cradle with lullabies wild;
I am here with the Wind—because I am his child."

—LUCY LARCOM

1. The windflower is another name for the anemone (a-nem´-o-ne). It is one of the earliest flowers of the spring; have you seen it?
2. Explain the meaning of this poem.

3. Look in the dictionary for the meaning of *boisterous, fragile, raiment.*

Note: Notice that "windflower" is composed of two words, *wind* and *flower*.   Such a word is called a compound word.

Note: Some compound words are written with a hyphen between the two words; as, *good-bye*.

4. Find in the poem other compound words that are written without the hyphen.

Note: The names of numbers under one hundred, that are expressed by two words, are written as compound words, as, *thirty-five, sixty-four*.

5. Copy ten compound words from your reader or other books.   Notice whether the words are written with or without the hyphen.

LESSON 120

PROSE STUDY—A PLANT

I dropped a seed into the earth.   It grew, and the plant was mine.

It was a wonderful thing, this plant of mine.   I did not know its name, and the plant did not bloom.   All I know is that I planted something apparently as lifeless as a grain of sand, and there came forth a green and living thing unlike the seed, unlike the soil in which it stood, unlike the air into which it grew. No one could tell me why it grew or how. It had secrets all its own, secrets that baffle the wisest men; yet this plant was my friend. It faded when I withheld the light, it wilted when I neglected to give it water, it flourished when I supplied its simple needs. One week I went away on a vacation; when I returned the plant was dead; and I missed it.

Although my little plant had died so soon, it had taught me a lesson; and the lesson is that it is worth while to have a plant.

—From *The Nature Study Idea*, by L. H. BAILEY

1. Write a story of "The Child and the Plant." Begin it in this way:
   A child found a seed that was apparently as lifeless as a grain of sand _____.
2. What were some of the secrets of the plant?
3. What was the lesson that the plant taught?
4. Why is it "worth while to have a plant"?
5. Find the meaning of *baffle, neglected, apparently.*
6. Tell the history of the plant.
7. Use some of the expressions from the prose study above.

LESSON 121

CONVERSATION—FLOWERS

1. Write answers to the following, each sentence to contain a series of words and but one connecting word with each series:

A. Name some flowers that grow wild.

B. Name the flowers that bloom earliest in the   spring, in your neighborhood.

C. Name some flowers that bloom in the fall.

D. Name some flowers that grow from seeds.

E. Name some flowers that grow from bulbs.

F. Name some flowers that grow on vines.

G. Name some flowers that grow on small plants.

H. Name some flowers that grow on bushes and shrubs.

I. Name some flowers that grow on trees.

J. Name some flowers that are fragrant.

K. Name some flowers that grow well in gardens.

L. What flowers do you like best?

2. Write a short description of your favorite flower.

LESSON 122

COMPOSITION—THE MONARCH BUTTERFLY

A beautiful orange and black butterfly flew slowly over the meadow. Near a milkweed stalk it paused and lighted on one of the tender green leaves. After a while it flew away, but on the milkweed it had left a number of tiny eggs.

Finish the story. Tell of the hatching of one of the eggs, the caterpillar, its growth and food, the chrysalis, and the butterfly.

LESSON 123

DICTATION

No one can travel far in England without observing with delight its universal verdure. This cannot be too highly praised. When other lands are white with dust, the fields of England are fresh and moist, and all its wealth of foliage is undimmed. In summer the entire island seems to be covered with a beautiful green carpet, of which the hedges, trees, and flowers are the figured patterns. The rustic houses veil themselves with vines, wild roses twine above the porches, and honeysuckles climb to the eaves.

—STODDARD'S LECTURES

1. Find the meaning of the following words and use them in sentences: "universal," "verdure," "foliage," "rustic," "moist."
2. What pictures does the paragraph suggest?
3. In the third sentence, with what are the fields of England contrasted?
4. How could the hedges, trees, and flowers suggest the patterns of a carpet?
5. Write the paragraph from dictation.
6. Complete the following sentences:
   A. "No" begins with a capital, because _____.
   B. "England" begins with a capital, because ____.
   C. There is a period after "verdure," because___.
   D. _____ and _____ describe "carpet."
   E. There is a comma after "hedges," because___.
   F. _____ describes houses.
   G. _____ describes roses.
   H. There are an apostrophe and s after Stoddard, because _____.
   I. "Stoddard" begins with a capital, because____.

LESSON 124

SELECTION FOR STUDY

October's Bright Blue Weather

Sun and skies and clouds of June,
    And flowers of June together,
Ye cannot rival for one hour
    October's bright blue weather;

When loud the bumblebee makes haste,
    Belated, thriftless vagrant,
And goldenrod is dying fast,
    And lanes with grapes are fragrant;

When gentians roll their fingers tight
    To save them for the morning,
And chestnuts fall from satin burrs
    Without a sound of warning;

When on the ground red apples lie
    In piles like jewels shining,
And redder still on old stone walls
    Are leaves of woodbine twining;

When all the lovely wayside things
    Their white-winged seeds are sowing,
And in the fields, still green and fair,
    Late aftermaths are growing;

When springs run low, and on the brooks,
    In idle golden freighting,

Bright leaves sink noiseless in the hush
Of woods, for winter waiting;

When comrades seek sweet country haunts,
By twos and twos together,
And count like misers, hour by hour,
October's bright blue weather.

O sun and skies and flowers of June,
Count all your boasts together,
Love loveth best of all the year
October's bright blue weather.

—HELEN HUNT JACKSON

1. Explain what is meant by the first stanza.
2. Why are apples compared to jewels?
3. What flowers are mentioned in this poem?
4. What seeds are referred to in the fifth stanza?
5. What fruits are mentioned?
6. Why does it speak of *satin burrs*?
7. Write a description of a picture that you would
   paint, if you were an artist, to illustrate this poem.
   Tell what you would have for the principal object,
   what you would place in the foreground, and what
   in the background.   Begin your description thus:
       If I were painting a picture to illustrate this
   poem, I would _____.

LESSON 125

CORRECT USE OF WORDS

A. Don't you like cold weather?
B. I don't like it very well.
C. Sam likes it; he doesn't mind the cold.

1. What contractions are used in the sentences?
2. For what words do they stand?

**Note: Use *don't* only in place of *do not*.
Use *doesn't* only in place of *does not*.**

3. Copy the following sentences, using the contractions in place of *do not* and *does not:*
   A. Bees do not work in winter.
   B. A bee does not have time to play.
   C. Do you not like October?
   D. The leaves do not remain on the trees all winter.
   E. The water in the brook does not sing as it did last summer.
   F. The goldenrod does not blossom until late in the summer.
   G. Some birds do not go south for the winter.
4. Write three questions beginning with *don't*.
5. Write three questions beginning with *doesn't*.

LESSON 126

PICTURE STUDY—THE BALLOON

This picture was painted by a French artist, Julien Dupre´, and represents country life in France.

1. Look at the picture and tell what you think the people are doing.
2. What do you suppose they are saying?
3. What were they doing before they saw the balloon?
4. What time of year is it?
5. Give a reason for your answer.
6. Compare this method of haying with that employed on a farm in the United States.
7. Describe the background of the picture. What kind of trees do you see?
8. Write a short description of the picture.

LESSON 127

COMPOSITION

1. Read again the poem, "October's Bright Blue Weather." Choose another month or season, and write a short article in which you try to prove that it is the most delightful time of the year.

From a painting by Dupre´
THE BALLOON

LESSON 128

CONVERSATION—SHIPS OF THE AIR

1. Tell what you can of airships and balloons.
2. What causes the balloon to rise?
3. How is the balloon affected by the wind?
4. Can it sail against the wind?
5. What is the motive power of an airship?
6. Can it sail against the wind?
7. If you have seen an airship, describe it.
8. Bring pictures to class.

LESSON 129

COMPOSITION—A TRIP IN AN AIRSHIP

1. Imagine yourself in an airship taking a trip over some country that you have studied recently in geography.
2. Tell of your start, how you felt as the airship went higher, what you saw as you looked over the sides.
3. Describe the mountains, rivers, cities, and people.
4. Stop at the place that interests you most.

LESSON 130

ABBREVIATIONS

The names of states are often abbreviated.

Alabama, AL	Missouri, MO
Alaska, AK	Montana, MT
Arizona, AZ	Nebraska, NE
Arkansas, AR	Nevada, NV
California, CA	New Hampshire, NH
Colorado, CO	New Jersey, NJ
Connecticut, CT	New Mexico, NM
Delaware, DE	New York, NY
District of Columbia, DC	North Carolina, NC
Florida, FL	North Dakota, ND
Georgia, GA	Ohio, OH
Hawaii, HI	Oklahoma, OK
Idaho, ID	Oregon, OR
Illinois, IL	Pennsylvania, PA
Indiana, IN	Rhode Island, RI
Iowa, IA	South Carolina, SC
Kansas, KS	South Dakota, SD
Kentucky, KY	Tennessee, TN
Louisiana, LA	Texas, TX
Maine, ME	Utah, UT
Maryland, MD	Virginia, VA
Massachusetts, MA	Vermont, VT
Michigan, MI	Washington, WA
Minnesota, MN	West Virginia, WV
Mississippi, MS	Wisconsin, WI

Wyoming, WY

1. Why are words sometimes abbreviated?
2. Learn the abbreviations.
3. Write them from dictation.

LESSON 131

REPRODUCTION—A FABLE

A cat and a monkey were one day warming themselves by a fire. The monkey found some chestnuts which he put into the fire to roast.

When the chestnuts were roasted, the monkey suggested that the cat should pull them out of the fire. The cat tried but burned her paw. The monkey praised her and urged her to try again, telling her that her paw was perfect for the job. This pleased the vain Puss; she tried again, and again burned her paw.

The monkey continued to flatter her, and foolish Puss at last succeeded in getting three chestnuts out of the fire, although her paws were badly burned. She said she would eat those three and not try to get any more. But the monkey had already cracked and eaten them.

The monkey said he did not know of anything better fitted for pulling chestnuts out of a fire than a foolish cat's paw.

1. Write this fable in dialogue form. Add to the conversation anything that will increase the interest. Begin in this way:

Monkey: Here is a good fire. Let us sit by it.

Cat: I like to sit by a fire.

LESSON 132

COMPOSITION

1. Tell or write one of the following stories:
   A. *Little Red Riding Hood*
   B. *Puss in Boots*
   C. *Cinderella*
   D. *Jack and the Bean Stalk*
   E. *The Sleeping Beauty*
   F. *Diamonds and Toads*
   G. *The Fisherman and his Wife*
   H. *The Tinder Box*
   I. *Beauty and the Beast*
   J. *The Ugly Duckling*
   K. *Why the Sea is Salt*
   L. *The Discontented Pine Tree*

If you do not know any of these, tell or write some other story.

LESSON 133

SELECTION FOR STUDY

THE GREEK MYTH—ECHO

According to Greek mythology, once upon a time, long, long ago, there was a beautiful girl whose name was Echo. She was fond of roaming through the woods and meadows, and among the rocks on the mountain side. She was fond of sports, too, and whenever there was a hunt or a contest of any kind, Echo was sure to be there.

But the girl had one great fault—she talked too much and often mimicked people in a rude and unkind way. One day, Juno, the ancient Greek mythical queen of the heavens, came down to the earth, searching for one of the gods.

She saw Echo picking flowers, and she called, "Do you know where he is, Echo?"

"He is Echo?" answered the saucy girl. "Who is Echo? I am Echo."

"What do you mean?" cried Juno.

"You mean, ha, ha, ha!" replied Echo, and, tossing her flowers high into the air, she ran up the hillside.

Juno was angry.

"Rude girl," she called, "you have dared too much. This shall be your punishment: Never again shall you speak except to repeat the last words of some other person."

Echo wandered from cave to cave, through valleys and among the mountain peaks. She grew thinner and thinner, until at last there was nothing left of her but a voice.

The voice still lives in the haunts of Echo, and repeats the last words of all who pass.

1. Tell the story of *Echo*.

Note: In the second paragraph the words "the Greek mythical queen of the heavens" explain who Juno was. Such a group of words is called an *explanatory expression*.

2. How is the explanatory expression separated from the rest of the sentence?

3. Find explanatory expressions in Lessons 1, 21, and 28.

LESSON 134

EXPLANATORY EXPRESSIONS

1. Use the following in sentences:

A. Jack, the boy who climbed the bean stalk

B. June, the month of roses

C. Cotton, the principal product of the Southern States

D. Mr. Carter, our new neighbor

E. Sir Edwin Landseer, the artist

F. Henry Wadsworth Longfellow, the best-loved poet of America

2. Place an explanatory expression after each of the following, and use in sentences:
A. George Washington
B. The President of the United States
C. Cinderella
D. Electricity
E. The Panama Canal
F. My friend

LESSON 135

SELECTION TO BE MEMORIZED

Summer or winter, day or night,
The woods are ever a new delight;
They give us peace, and they make us strong,
Such wonderful balms to them belong;
So, living or dying, I'll take my ease
Under the trees, under the trees.

—RICHARD HENRY STODDARD

1. Write the selection from memory.
2. Bring leaves from different kinds of trees.
3. Name them and tell which trees are favorites as shade trees.
4. Name some trees that are valuable for timber and for fuel.
5. At what season are trees the most beautiful?

LESSON 136

SINGULAR AND PLURAL

A. pony	E. ponies
B. story	F. stories
C. lady	G. ladies
D. sky	H. skies

1. Study the words.
2. With what letter does each word in the singular end?
3. Is the letter before the last letter a vowel or a consonant?
4. What change was made in forming the plural?
5. Write the plural of the following words:

A. balcony	F. cherry
B. family	G. study
C. country	H. city
D. daisy	I. sky
E. baby	J. enemy

6. Copy the following sentence, filling the blanks to make a rule for this formation of the plural:
   Note: Words ending in _____ preceded by a _____ form the plural by changing _____ to _____ and adding _____.

LESSON 137

PICTURE STUDY—A RIVER SCENE

There once lived in France a boy who thought springtime the most beautiful season of the year. He was never so happy as when wandering through the woods or by the edge of the river that was near his home. The boy's name was Jean Camille Corot (kə-ɛrō). When he grew older he became an artist, and he put upon canvas the beautiful scenes he loved so well.

1. Here is a copy of one his pictures. Notice how beautifully the trees have been painted.
2. Did the artist wish the landscape, or the people, to be the more prominent?
3. Can you think of any reason why there is little ground and much sky in the picture? Which would make the better background for beautiful trees?
4. What can you see in the distance?
5. Does the picture suggest morning or evening?
6. Would such a place attract you? What would you do if you were there?
7. Can you find a quotation that this picture would illustrate?

From a painting by Corot

A RIVER SCENE

LESSON 138

DICTATION

Jean Corot, the artist, once said:
After one of my excursions I invite nature to come
and spend a few days with me. Pencil in hand, I hear
the birds singing, the trees rustling in the wind; I see the
running brooks and the streams charged with a thousand
reflections of sky and earth—nay, the very sun rises and
sets in my studio.

1. Explain the meaning of the paragraph.
2. If a picture were made to illustrate it, what
would the picture contain?
3. Write the quotation from dictation.

LESSON 139

SELECTION FOR STUDY

THE SONG OF THE BROOK

I come from haunts of coot and hern,
I make a sudden sally,
And sparkle out among the fern,
To bicker down a valley.

By thirty hills I hurry down,
Or slip between the ridges,
By twenty thorps, a little town,
And half a hundred bridges.

I chatter over stony ways,
    In little sharps and trebles,
I bubble into eddying bays,
    I babble on the pebbles.

With many a curve my banks I fret
    By many a field and fallow,
And many a fairy foreland set
    With willow-weed and mallow.

I chatter, chatter, as I flow
    To join the brimming river,
For men may come and men may go,
    But I go on forever.
*   *   *   *
I steal by lawns and grassy plots,
    I slide by hazel covers;
I move the sweet forget-me-nots
    That grow for happy lovers.
I slip, I slide, I gloom, I glance,
    Among my skimming swallows;
I make the netted sunbeam dance
    Against my sandy shallows.
*   *   *   *
And out again I curve and flow
    To join the brimming river,
For men may come and men may go,
    But I go on forever.

                  —ALFRED TENNYSON

1. What is meant by the first line of the poem?
2. Explain the second line.
3. Why does the poet use the word "chatter," in the third stanza? Suggest other words that might have been used instead.
4. What is meant by "brimming river," in the fifth stanza?
5. What season does this poem suggest?
6. What is the meaning of the seventh stanza?
7. Name some of the places through which the brook passed.
8. Which stanza suggests the prettiest picture?
9. Would "A River Scene," by Corot, fit a part of this poem? Describe some other picture of a river or stream.
10. Have you seen a brook like this? Describe it.
11. Memorize the stanza you like best, and also the last stanza.

LESSON 140

COMPOSITION

1. The Missouri River has its source in the mountains of Yellowstone National Park. With the aid of a map, trace a drop of water from Yellowstone National Park to the Gulf of Mexico. Begin your story in this way:

THE STORY A DROP OF WATER TOLD

For days I floated high above the earth in a soft fleecy cloud. Then the air became colder, and I fell down from the blue sky to the side of a mountain in a wonderful park.

2. Read again "The Song of the Brook," Lesson 139. If possible use some of the following expressions in your story: "over stony ways," "brimming river," "grassy plots," "sandy shallows," "down a valley."

3. Use other expressions from the poem.

LESSON 141

BUSINESS LETTERS

3042 GRAND AVE.
ST. LOUIS, MO
Sept. 20, 1914

G. B. HARDIN & SON
FLORAL PARK, OHIO
GENTLEMEN:

Please send me one dozen tulip bulbs as advertised on page 65 of your 1914 catalogue. I enclose a money order for one dollar and fifty cents ($1.50) to pay for them.

Yours respectfully,
JOHN EDWARDS.

FLORAL PARK, OHIO
Sept. 22, 1914

MR. JOHN EDWARDS
3042 GRAND AVE.
ST. LOUIS, MO
DEAR SIR:

Your communication of Sept. 20 with money order for one dollar and fifty cents ($1.50) has been received. We have filed your order and will ship the bulbs at the earliest possible date.

Awaiting your further orders, we remain,
Yours truly,
G. B. HARDIN & SON

Note: The part of the letter between the heading and the salutation is called the address. It consists of the name and place of business of the person or firm to whom the letter is written.

1. Write the letters from dictation.

LESSON 142

LETTER WRITING

1. Write to the publishers for a copy of this book or some other book that they publish. State that you enclosed a money order in payment.

2. Write a reply stating that your order has been received, and that the book has been sent.

LESSON 143

AUTOBIOGRAPHY OF A BOOK

1. Trace a book from the time it left the printers with its clean, fresh pages and stiff, strong back. Tell who bought the book, how it was treated, and what different people read it.
2. Imagine that you are the book, and write its autobiography, as you wrote your own.

LESSON 144

CORRECT USE OF WORDS

1. What is a homonym? (See Lesson 110.)
2. Find the meanings of the following homonyms, and use each in a sentence:

A. do	E. to	I. sew
dew	two	sow
due	too	so
B. grate	F. week	J. bee
great	weak	be
C. dear	G. right	K. fir
deer	write	fur
D. nose	H. rein	L. new
knows	rain	knew

LESSON 145

A DIARY

Thursday, Sept. 14, 1843. This morning I ran in the wind and played be a horse and had a lovely time with Anna and Lizzie. We were fairies, and made gowns and paper wings. It rained when I went to bed and made a pretty noise on the roof.

Oct. 8. When I woke the first thought I got was, "It's Mother's birthday; I must be very good." I ran and wished her a happy birthday and gave her my kiss. After breakfast we gave her our presents. I had a moss cross and a piece of poetry for her.

We did not have any school, and played in the woods and got red leaves. In the evening we danced and sang, and I read a story about "Contentment."

Oct. 20. I rose at five, and after breakfast washed the dishes, and then helped Mother work.

Anna is in Boston with Cousin Louisa. I took care of Abby in the afternoon, and in the evening I made some pretty things for my dolly.

Nov. 5. Did my lessons, and in the evening Mother read "Kenilworth" to us while we sewed. It is splendid! We have had a lovely day. All the trees were covered with ice and it shone like diamonds or fairy palaces.

—*From the Diary of* LOUISA M. ALCOTT

Note: People often keep a record of the events of each day. This record is called a diary.

1. Keep a diary for a week. Put down every day the events that interest you, or that you would like to remember.

2. Complete the following sentences:

A. There is a period after *Sept.*, because _____.

B. There is an apostrophe in *it's*, because _____.

C. *Mother's* is written with an apostrophe and s, because _____.

D. Anna begins with a capital letter, because _____.

E. *Cousin* begins with a capital letter, because _____.

LESSON 146

LONGFELLOW'S DIARY

Henry Wadsworth Longfellow put into his diary bits of beautiful description. The following was written June 23, 1831:

I can almost fancy myself in Spain, the morning is so soft and beautiful. The tessellated shadow of the honeysuckle lies motionless upon my study floor, as if it were a figure in the carpet; and through the open window comes the fragrance of the wild brier and the mock orange. The birds are caroling in the trees, and their shadows flit across the window as they dart to and fro in the sunshine, while the murmur of the bee, the cooing of the doves from the eaves, and the whirring of a little hummingbird that has its nest in the honeysuckle, send up a sound of joy to meet the rising sun.

1. Find, in the dictionary, the meaning of the word "tessellated."
2. Read the description several times. Notice the beginning and the close.
3. Using this as a model, describe an autumn day, a spring day, or a winter day.

LESSON 147

SELECTION FOR STUDY

THE CLOUD

I bring fresh showers for the thirsting flowers,
    From the seas and the streams;
I bear light shade for the leaves when laid
    In their noonday dreams.

From my wings are shaken the dews that waken
    The sweet buds every one,
When rocked to rest on their mother's breast,
    As she dances about the sun.

I wield the flail of the lashing hail,
  And whiten the green plains under;
And then again I dissolve it in rain,
  And laugh as I pass in thunder.

I sift the snow on the mountains below,
  And their great pines groan aghast;
And all the night 'tis my pillow white,
  While I sleep in the arms of the blast.
                    —Percy Bysshe Shelley

1. What does the cloud do for the flowers?
2. Explain the third line of the first stanza.
3. What things are mentioned in the third and fourth stanzas, that the cloud does?
4. Explain the meaning of "flail," "dissolve," "groan," "aghast," "blast."
5. What is the meaning of the second line of the fourth stanza?
6. What is the meaning of the third and fourth lines of the fourth stanza?
7. Which lines in each stanza of this poem rhyme?
8. Find two words in the first line that rhyme.
9. Find two words in the third line that rhyme.
   Note: Such rhymes are called *interior* rhymes.
10. Find other interior rhymes in this poem.

11. Find other poems containing interior rhymes.
12. Write a stanza of four lines in which the first and third, or the second and fourth lines rhyme.
13. Let your poem be about one of the following:
    A. A brook or river
    B. A valley
    C. The picture, *A River Scene*
    D. A snowstorm
    E. Some part of the description by Longfellow, Lesson 146
14. Write another stanza, choosing any subject you wish

LESSON 148

DICTATION—A DRY SEASON

It is a long time since much rain fell. The ground is a little dry; the road is a good deal dusty. The garden bakes. Transplanted trees are thirsty. Wheels are shrinking and tires are looking dangerous. Men speculate on the clouds; they begin to calculate how long it will be, if no rain falls, before the potatoes will suffer; the oats, the grass, the corn—everything!

—HENRY WARD BEECHER

1. Write the paragraph from dictation.

LESSON 149

COMPOSITION

1. Study the paragraph quoted in Lesson 148. Notice the form of the description. Write a paragraph entitled "A Wet Season." Begin the paragraph in this way:

Rain, rain, rain! All day and all night it rained steadily. It _____.

LESSON 150

SUMMARY—Continued from Lesson 100

To Remember

Words that are alike in sound but different in meaning are call homonyms.

The name of God and all words referring to the Deity should begin with capitals.

An explanatory expression should be separated from the rest of the sentence by commas.

Use *don't* only in place of *do not*.

Use *doesn't* only in place of *does not*.

Words ending in *y* preceded by a consonant form the plural by changing *y* to *i* and adding *es*.

Words ending in *f* or *fe* form the plural by changing *f* or *fe* to *ves*.

LESSON 151

CORRECT USE OF WORDS

1. Use the following in sentences:
   A. he and I
   B. she and I
   C. you and I
   D. from you and me
   E. by you and me
   F. with you and me
   G. to him and me
   H. with them and me
2. When you speak of yourself and one or more others, whom do you mention last?

LESSON 152

PICTURE STUDY—TWO MOTHERS

1. What do you see in the picture?
2. Why is the picture called *Two Mothers*?
3. How does the mother care for her little girl?
4. How does the hen care for her chicks?
5. Does the hen seem to talk to her chickens?
6. How does she warn them of danger?
7. How does she feed them?
8. What do you think the child is saying?

From a painting by Elizabeth Gardner
Two Mothers

LESSON 153

COMPOSITION—AN IMPORTANT EVENT

1. Do you read the newspapers?
2. Study carefully the form in which an important piece of news is presented. Does the article give the opinion of the writer or merely state facts? Notice the headlines. What do they contain?
3. Imagine that you are a newspaper reporter and write an article about the most important event of the past month. Give headlines.
4. Was the event of importance to your neighborhood alone, or to the state and country?

LESSON 154

SELECTION FOR STUDY

THE TREE

The Tree's early leaf-buds were bursting their brown;
"Shall I take them away?" said the Frost, sweeping
    down.
      "No, leave them alone
      Till the blossoms have grown,"
Prayed the Tree, while he trembled from rootlet to
    crown.
The Tree bore his blossoms and all the birds sung;

"Shall I take them away?" said the Wind as he swung.
　　"No, leave them alone
　　Till the berries have grown,"
Said the Tree while his leaflets quivering hung.

The Tree bore his fruit in the midsummer glow:
Said the girl, "May I gather thy berries now?"
　　"Yes, all thou canst see;
　　Take them; all are for thee,"
Said the Tree while he bent down his laden boughs low.

　　　　　　　　　—BJÖRNSTJERNE BJÖRNSON

1. Write the first stanza of the poem from memory.
2. With what kind of letter does the word "Tree" begin?

   Note: When animals or objects are represented as talking and acting like people, they are said to be "personified."

   Note:　The name of anything personified should begin with a capital letter.
3. Find in the poem other objects that are personified.
4. Find in the poem an example of the possessive singular.
5. Write lists of the words that rhyme.

LESSON 155

COMPOSITION

1. Tell the story of an oak desk in your schoolroom. Begin your story in this way:

   Once upon a time a tiny acorn fell to the ground near the foot of a great mountain.

   Tell about—

   A. The growth of the oak tree
   B. The cutting of the tree
   C. Hauling the log to the river
   D. Floating down the river to the mill
   E. Sawing the log
   F. The making of the desk
   G. Selling the desk
   H. What has happened to it since it came to your school
   I. Descriptions of the woods where the tree grew
   J. The river

LESSON 156

COMPOSITION—A STORY

Carl Bremen, who lived with his parents in a little house on the side of a mountain, discovered one morning that the heavy rain had washed away part of the railroad track.

1. Complete the story, telling how Carl warned the train, why the engineer did not at first see him, what the passengers said, and what they did for him.

LESSON 157

A DIALOGUE

Suppose that a rich man, Mr. Evans, who was on the train, became interested in Carl and offered to take the boy into his home and give him an education.

1. Write the dialogue that might have taken place between the two, in which Mr. Evans asks questions concerning Carl's home and finds out that the boy longs for a chance to go to school.

Begin the dialogue in this way:

Mr. Evans: My boy, you have done a brave deed. Had it not been for you many of us would have lost our lives. Where is your home?

Carl: _____ _____.

LESSON 158

LETTER WRITING

1. Write a letter which Carl might have sent to his mother, telling about his new home and his school.

LESSON 159

FORMATION OF SENTENCES

A. A brave boy saved the train.

B. He lived in a little house on the side of the mountain.

C. A brave boy who lived in a little house on the side of the mountain saved the train. (Notice that the two sentences above were joined by the word *who.*)

1. Combine the sentences of each of the following groups by using the word *who:*

A. The passengers crowded about the boy.

B. They had been saved.

A. A rich man took the boy to his home.

B. The rich man was on the train.

A. The artist was Jean Corot.

B. He painted beautiful pictures of trees.

A. The people are called Eskimos.

B. They live in the far north.

A. The fisherman came home before the storm.

B. He had been out to sea.

A. The people saw a balloon high in the air.

B. They were working in the fields.

A. The man waited to see what would happen.
B. He placed the stone in the road.
A. The boy found a sack of gold.
B. He moved the stone from the road.

LESSON 160

COMPOSITION—A STORY

1. Write a story about a man who is rich but who has no little boys or girls in his home. As he passes down the street on a cold night, he sees a poor little ragged boy gazing wistfully into a shop window filled with toys.
2. Tell what the man did for the boy.

LESSON 161

LETTER WRITING

1. Write to W. A. King, a real estate dealer in Erie, PA, telling him that you expect to move to that city and wish to rent a house.
2. Tell him the size of the house that you will need, and what rent you are willing to pay.
3. Write the reply, in which the real estate dealer describes a house which he has for rent, and states the price.

LESSON 162

PICTURE STUDY—SUMMER EVENING

1. What in the picture suggests the title?
2. Have you seen places in the country similar to this?
3. Which part of the picture is the center of interest?
4. Does the dress of the woman tell anything about her?
5. What do you see on the other bank of the river?
6. What is in the far distance?
7. If you were to add to the picture, what would you put to the right? In front? To the left?
8. Write a short description of a summer evening.

LESSON 163

STUDY OF WORDS

1. Make a list of twelve or more words that tell of size, weight, height, or depth; as, gigantic, extensive, tiny.
2. Which words in your list describe the following: A. mountain B. river C. tree D. plain E. flower F. man G. valley H. cloud
3. Write sentences containing the various words of your list.

SUMMER EVENING

From a painting by Adam

LESSON 164

SELECTION FOR STUDY

WOODMAN, SPARE THAT TREE

Woodman, spare that tree!
    Touch not a single bough!
In youth it sheltered me,
    And I'll protect it now.
'Twas my forefather's hand
    That placed it near his cot;
There, woodman, let it stand,
    Thy axe shall harm it not!

That old familiar tree,
    Whose glory and renown
Are spread o'er land and sea—
    And wouldst thou hew it down?
Woodman, forbear thy stroke!
    Cut not its earth-bound ties,
Oh, spare that aged oak,
    Now towering to the skies!

When but an idle boy
    I sought its grateful shade;
In all their gushing joy
    Here, too, my sisters played.
My mother kissed me here;
    My father pressed my hand—

Forgive this foolish tear,
   But let that old oak stand!

My heartstrings round thee cling,
   Close as thy bark, old friend!
Here shall the wild bird sing,
   And still thy branches bend.
Old tree, the storm still brave!
   And, woodman, leave the spot;
While I've a hand to save,
   Thy axe shall harm it not.

                    —GEORGE POPE MORRIS

1. Describe a picture that would illustrate the first stanza of the poem.
2. Why does the author wish to protect the tree?
3. Read the lines that show why the tree was dear to the poet.
4. Explain the first and second lines of the fourth stanza.
5. Find in the poem examples of the following:
   A. Person spoken to
   B. Contractions
   C. Possessive form
   D. Plurals formed by adding *s* to the singular
   E. Plurals formed by adding *es* to the singular

LESSON 165

COMPOSITION—A PLEA FOR LIFE

A great oak tree has stood for more than a century near a busy street. Now a building is to be erected there, and the tree must be cut down.

Imagine that you are the tree, and write a plea for your life. Tell how you have grown from a tiny acorn, how your shade has protected people from the sun, and how the birds have built nests in your branches. Let the last paragraph beg for continued life.

LESSON 166

REVIEW—SINGULAR AND PLURAL

Copy the following words, and write after each its plural form:

loaf	lady	insect	church	century
knife	family	worm	farmer	potato
brush	man	deer	child	fairy
goose	word	wolf	country	cricket
fox	cow	city	eagle	mouse
crow	ox	robin	thief	daisy
field	calf	bench	box	wife
sky	echo	meadow	arch	woman
sheep	basket	bough	sister	man
branch	storm	baby	box	paragraph

LESSON 167

KINDS OF SENTENCES

A. Do not cut down that great tree.
B. It has stood for many years.
C. Birds have built their nests in its branches.
D. Do you not see how strong it is?
E. Will you not stop and rest in its shade?
F. Put away your axe.
G. The tree is saved!
H. Long live the great tree!

1. Which of these sentences ask questions?
   Note: A sentence that asks a question is called an *interrogative* sentence.
2. Which sentences command or request?
   Note: A sentence that commands or requests is called an *imperative* sentence.
3. Which sentences exclaim?
   Note: A sentence that exclaims, or is introduced by *what* or *how* (not asking questions), is called an *exclamatory* sentence.
4. Which sentences state something?
   Note: A sentence that states something is a *declarative* sentence.

5. Write three declarative sentences about the picture on page 146.
6. Write three interrogative sentences about the picture on page 103.
7. Write three exclamatory sentences suggested by the picture on page 83.
8. Write three imperative sentences that command.
9. Write three imperative sentences that make requests.

LESSON 168

LETTER WRITING

1. Write one of the following letters, and the reply:
   A. Henry Andrews, who lives at Hickory Grove, Iowa, R. D. 4, writes to Barnett Bros., 854 State Street, Chicago, IL, asking the cost of a box of tools; he states what he wishes the box to contain.
   B. Mrs. Ethel Edwards, who lives at Forestville, ME, writes to Cooper Dry Goods Co., Portland, ME, asking the price of a set of furs; she states what kind of furs she prefers.
   Note: In the reply to this letter the salutation should be *Dear Madam.*

LESSON 169

SELECTION FOR STUDY

LEGEND OF THE ARBUTUS

Far, far away in the Northland, in a wigwam made of deerskins, there once lived an old, old man. It was winter. The pine trees and the firs were loaded with thick coverings of snow; the streams were silent under their coating of ice; no bird or animal was to be seen. It was very cold.

Inside the lodge the old man fanned the few sparks of his tiny fire, and tried to coax them into a bright flame. Day after day he sat there, and day after day the fire became smaller and smaller.

Many weeks passed, and then one day the tent flap was opened, and a beautiful maiden entered the wigwam. Her cheeks were as rosy as the skies at dawn, her eyes were as tender and bright as the starlight, and on her brown hair she wore a wreath of flowers that were pink and sweet.

"Who are you?" cried the old man, "And why do you come? Do you not know that it is winter?"

The maiden laughed, and as she did so the air in the tent became warm and fragrant.

"Do you not know who I am?" continued the old man. "When I breathe, the waters of the brooks and lakes become still and dead; the flowers die, and the robins fly away to the Southland."

With a smile the maiden answered, "When I breathe, the brooks murmur and laugh, the lakes sparkle in the sunshine, sweet blossoms cover the earth, and the birds come back to build their nests in the tree tops."

"When I nod my head," said the old man, "snow covers the ground, the north wind blows, and it is bitter cold."

"When I nod my head," said the maiden, "the warm rain falls, the south wind sends its gentle zephyrs, and all the earth is glad."

The old man answered not; he sank slowly to the ground, for his eyes were heavy with sleep. Tenderly the maiden brushed aside his snow-white tresses, and gently she placed some of her flowers of pink and white in his bosom.

"Alas!" she said, "Poor old Winter, you do not love the beauty that I have brought, you do not know that I am Spring."

As she paused, the wigwam, the fire, and the old man seemed to disappear; but where the old man had lain was a mass of thick leaves from which peeped flowers that were pink and white and beautiful.

"See!" cried the maiden, "Here is the arbutus, the first sweet flower of Spring. Whoever picks you shall know that Winter, with his snow, his ice, and his cold north wind, has gone, and that gentle Spring is near."

1. Tell the story of the "Legend of the Arbutus."
2. Make a list of the pictures that might be used to illustrate this story. Write a short description of one of them.
3. Find in the story four different ways in which capital letters are used.

LESSON 170
CONVERSATION—THE POST OFFICE

1. What is done to the envelope at the post office, before the letter is sent?
2. Why must every envelope bear a stamp?
3. What are the duties of a postman? How does he carry the mail? At what time of the year are his burdens heaviest?
4. If the postman cannot find the person to whom the letter belongs, what is done with it?
5. Tell what you can about *rural delivery*.
6. Tell what you can about *parcel post*.
7. What do you understand by *special delivery*.
8. What does it cost to send a letter by special delivery?
9. How may money be sent safely by mail?
10. What do you understand by *registered mail?*

11. Trace a letter sent from your home to 654 Broadway, New York, NY.
12. At least how many people would have to handle it before it reached its destination?

LESSON 171

DESCRIPTION—A POSTAGE STAMP

1. Examine different kinds of postage stamps.
2. Describe one of them. Tell what pictures and printing you find on it. Tell why you think the picture was chosen.
3. If you have any foreign stamps, compare them with those of the United States.

LESSON 172

TITLES

A. The children sang, "Home, Sweet Home."
B. "Black Beauty" is the story of a horse.
C. The subject of his composition was "Happy Days on the Farm."
D. Do you read "The Daily News?"
1. A. What book is named in these sentences?
   B. What composition? C. What song?
   D. What newspaper?

2. What marks enclose titles of poems, books, etc., when they are used in a sentence?

3. Do all the words in every title begin with capital letters?

Note: Titles of poems, books, etc., when used in a sentence are sometimes italicized.

4. Write sentences containing the name of—

    A. A song

    B. A poem

    C. A book you have read

    D. A book you wish to read

    E. A newspaper

    F. A subject for a composition

LESSON 173

LETTER WRITING

A. George Randall, Fremont, VA, writes to Mr. W. T. Blair of the Public Library of Richmond, VA, asking for a list of ten books suitable for boys to read.

(Such a letter should enclose a stamp for the answer.)

B. Edith Randall writes for a similar list of books for girls.

1. Write one of the letters, and a reply.

LESSON 174

SELECTION TO BE MEMORIZED

Neither a borrower nor a lender be;
For loan oft loses both itself and friend,
And borrowing dulls the edge of husbandry.
This above all: to thine own self be true,
And it must follow, as the night the day,
Thou canst not then be false to any man.

—WILLIAM SHAKESPEARE

1. How does a loan often lose "both itself and friend?"
2. Explain the third line.
3. Tell what you think the poet meant by the last two lines.
4. Memorize the poem.
5. Write the poem from memory.

LESSON 175

FORMATION OF SENTENCES

A. Two children went out to play in the new-fallen snow.

B. It was a cold winter day.

C. The sun shone after a long storm.

One cold winter day, when the sun shone after a long storm, two little children went out to play in the new-fallen snow.

1. Notice that the three short sentences were combined into one long one. Which form do you like better?

2. Combine each of the following groups into a single sentence; change some of the words if necessary:

   A. The south wind came to see what the storm had done. The south wind lives in the land of summer.

   B. He blew his soft breath against the snowflakes. The snowflakes disappeared.

   C. The elm tree stood by the gate. The elm tree shook its branches. The elm tree said, "I think spring has come; I must wake my buds."

   D. The seeds had slept all winter under the dead leaves. The seeds heard the south wind calling. The seeds said, "It must be time to rise; we hear the sounds of spring."

   E. The robin had been in the Southland. The robin heard the call of spring. The robin said, "I must go north again; it is time to build my nest."

3. Write five groups of short sentences and change each group to a single sentence.

From a painting by Boughton   RETURN OF THE MAYFLOWER

LESSON 176

PICTURE STUDY—RETURN OF THE MAYFLOWER

1. Tell what you can about the Pilgrims.
2. What was the name of the ship in which they came to America?
3. This picture represents the return of the ship to England.
4. Describe the picture.
5. Which are the principal figures?
6. What do you think must have been the feelings of the people who remained in America?

LESSON 177

LETTER WRITING

The captain of the *Mayflower* carried many letters which the people who remained in America had written to their friends and relatives in England. Imagine yourself a boy or girl who had come to America on the *Mayflower*, and write a letter to a cousin in England. Tell of the new country, the Indians, the hunting and fishing, and an incident that might happen in a child's life.

LESSON 178

SELECTION FOR STUDY

In 1812 a war broke out between the United States and England. The first sea fight was between the United States ship *Constitution* and the English man-of-war *Guerrière.*

The ships were thought to be about equal in fighting strength, but within half an hour the United States ship had won a splendid victory. The *Guerriere* was destroyed, while the *Constitution* was practically unharmed. Because of this and other victories which the *Constitution* won, the people called the *Constitution*, "Old Ironsides."

OLIVER WENDELL HOLMES

After many years of service she was pronounced unsound, and it was decided that she should be destroyed. Oliver Wendell Holmes opposed this plan, and wrote the poem, "Old Ironsides," which was copied in newspapers throughout the country. By means of this appeal the ship was saved and was afterwards used as a training ship for naval cadets.

OLD IRONSIDES

Aye, tear her tattered ensign down!
    Long has it waved on high,
And many an eye has danced to see
    That banner in the sky;
Beneath it rung the battle shout,
    And burst the cannon's roar;
The meteor of the ocean air
    Shall sweep the clouds no more.

Her deck, once red with heroes' blood,
    Where knelt the vanquished foe,
When winds were hurrying o'er the flood,
    And waves were white below,
No more shall feel the victor's tread,
    Or know the conquered knee;
The harpies of the shore shall pluck
    The eagle of the sea!

Oh, better that her shattered hulk
    Should sink beneath the wave;

Her thunders shook the mighty deep,
    And there should be her grave;
Nail to the mast her holy flag,
    Set every threadbare sail,
And give her to the god of storms,
    The lightning and the gale!

        —OLIVER WENDELL HOLMES

1. What is the meaning of "aye" and "ensign"?
2. Explain the third and fourth lines of the first stanza.
3. To what does the seventh line refer?
4. What is the meaning of "vanquished foe"?
5. In the third stanza explain "shattered hulk."
6. What did the poet think should be done with the ship?
7. Account for uses of the *apostrophe* in the poem.

LESSON 179

STUDY OF WORDS

The word *plot* means nearly the same as *plan*.
Note: Words that have the same or nearly the same meaning are called *synonyms*.
1. Find in column B a synonym for each word in column A; write the words in pairs, thus, *plot—plan*.

A	B
lessen	high
generous	sure
grand	busy
ancient	joy
industrious	old
courageous	misfortune
famous	magnificent
lofty	scold
splendid	quiet
scheme	celebrated
disaster	bold
happiness	superb
certain	liberal
censure	plot
silent	diminish

LESSON 180

DESCRIPTION OF AN OLD MILL

Near the waterfall where two roads meet, stands an old sawmill. Back of it rises a hill covered with thick underbrush; to the side of it splashes the clear blue water of the little river; while in front of it stands an immense oak tree whose broad branches stretch far above the old building at its base.

The mill is built of the lumber which its own saws cut; part of it was blown down in a big storm a few years ago and has never been replaced. Through many summers and winters the old mill has stood there: owners have come and have gone; boys who played around its open door and watched the whirring saws have grown to manhood and have moved away—but still the old mill stands.

Its interior is dark and dingy. Its walls are covered with cobwebs, which have caught particles of sawdust until they look like heavy woven curtains. But the saws are bright, and daily they cut the logs that the rippling river brings from far up among the hills.

The owner talks of improvements. He often speaks of repairing the damaged part and of replacing some of the broken windows, but the owner, like the mill itself, is old, and as the days pass the mill remains unchanged.

1. Does this description present a picture to you?
2. After reading the description could you recognize the old mill if you were to pass it?
3. Notice that in the first sentence the most important part is placed last. Rearrange the sentence so that this part shall be first. Do you like it as well? The first part of the sentence tells two things about the location of the mill.
4. Use the following groups of words as parts of sentences; let the first part of each sentence answer the question *where.* Write two or more statements about the location of each object that you are describing.

   A. —— stood a cherry tree covered with blossoms.
   B. ——was a ship that had fought many battles.
   C. ——sat an old man.
   D. ——a mocking bird had built its nest.
   E. ——lived a gray squirrel.
   F. ——was a row of stately birches.

LESSON 181
COMPOSITION—A DESCRIPTION

1. Read again the description of an old mill given in Lesson 180.

2. Use the following outline in describing one of the buildings in the list below:

A. Location
B. Surroundings
C. Material of which it is built
D. Age
E. Size
F. Interior
G. Incidents connected with the history of the buildings
H. Adaptation to purpose it serves
I. Improvements that might be made

Church   Library   Post Office
School   Store   Factory
     Railroad Station   Old Farmhouse

3. In some of your sentences place the important part last.

LESSON 182

DESCRIPTION OF A PERSON

1. Make an outline for the description of a person.
2. Use your outline in describing one of the following:

A. a tramp   C. a baby   E. a blacksmith
B. an engineer   D. a policeman F. your mother

LESSON 183

SELECTION TO BE MEMORIZED

The night has a thousand eyes,
    The day but one;
Yet the light of the bright world dies
    With the dying sun.

The mind has a thousand eyes,
    The heart but one;
Yet the light of a whole life dies
    When love is done.

—FRANCES BOURDILLON

1. What are the eyes of the night?
2. What is the eye of the day?
3. Explain the fifth line.
4. Memorize the poem.
5. Write the poem from memory.

LESSON 184

CORRECT USE OF WORDS

1. What are synonyms?
2. What are homonyms?
3. Use the following homonyms in sentences:

A. there	H. sent
their	cent
B. herd	scent
heard	I. fair
C. flour	fare
flower	J. o'er
D. sea	oar
see	K. be
E. here	bee
hear	L. stair
F. by	stare
buy	M. vale
G. hare	veil
hair	

LESSON 185

LETTER WRITING

Tom Evans writes to his uncle, George A. Evans, a rich man, calling attention to the condition of a poor family in the neighborhood.

1. Write the letter, telling about the family and their needs.

LESSON 186

COMPOSITION—A STORY

Early one morning, Harry Ford heard a noise on the back porch.

He opened the door and there on the steps was a poor little dog that held up a lame foot and cried pitifully.

1. Finish the story. Tell how Harry took care of the dog, what tricks he taught his pet, and what games they played together.
2. Let the last part of the story tell of something that the dog did for Harry, or for some member of his family.

LESSON 187

AN IMAGINARY DIARY

1. Review Lesson 145.
2. Write a diary of a Maltese kitten, for one week. Include in the diary something about—
   A. The kitten's home
   B. Its master or mistress
   C. Other pets in the family
   D. Some incident that might happen to a kitten

From a painting by Nicolas Maes
THE SPINNER

LESSON 188

PICTURE STUDY—THE SPINNER

1. Describe the picture.
2. Tell what you can of the processes of spinning and weaving used in early days.
3. How was the spindle used?
4. Of what use was the distaff?
5. Tell something of the manufacture of woolen goods at the present time.
6. Does the picture interest you?
7. Compare it with *The Gleaners*, page 210. In what ways are the pictures similar?
8. Why do you suppose an artist chose such a subject for a painting?
9. If the spinner had been a young woman, would the picture have been more pleasing?
10. Do such pictures make you feel more kindly toward the aged and poor?
11. Mention subjects that might be used for pictures to teach the same lesson.
12. Describe one of the pictures that you have suggested.

LESSON 189

SELECTION FOR STUDY

THE HERITAGE

The rich man's son inherits lands,
　　And piles of brick and stone and gold,
And he inherits soft white hands,
　　And tender flesh that fears the cold,
　　Nor dares to wear a garment old;
A heritage, it seems to me,
　　One scarce would wish to hold in fee.

The rich man's son inherits cares;
　　The bank may break, the factory burn,
A breath may burst his bubble shares,
　　And soft white hands could hardly earn
　　A living that would serve his turn;
A heritage, it seems to me,
　　One scarce would wish to hold in fee.

　　*　　　*　　　*　　　*　　　*

What doth the poor man's son inherit?
　　Stout muscles and a sinewy heart,
A hardy frame, a hardier spirit;
　　King of two hands, he does his part
　　In every useful toil and art;

A heritage, it seems to me,
A king might wish to hold in fee.

*   *   *   *   *

What doth the poor man's son inherit?
    A patience learned of being poor,
Courage, if sorrow come, to bear it,
    A fellow feeling that is sure
    To make the outcast bless his door;
A heritage, it seems to me,
A king might wish to hold in fee.

O rich man's son! There is a toil,
    That with all others level stands;
Large charity doth never soil,
    But only whitens soft white hands—
    This is the best crop from thy lands;
A heritage, it seems to me,
Worth being rich to hold in fee.

O poor man's son! Scorn not thy state,
    There is worse weariness than thine,
In merely being rich and great;
    Toil only gives the soul to shine,
    And makes rest fragrant and benign;
A heritage, it seems to me,
Worth being poor to hold in fee.

                         —JAMES RUSSELL LOWELL

Note: *To hold in fee* **means** *to possess.*

1. What is the meaning of "inherit," "heritage," "sinewy," "benign"?
2. What are the things that a rich man's son inherits?
3. Why do these things bring him cares?
4. What does a poor man's son inherit?
5. Tell in your own words the substance of the fourth stanza.
6. Explain, "A patience learned of being poor."
7. In the fifth stanza, what toil may the rich man's son possess?
8. What is meant by the second line of the sixth stanza?
9. Explain the fifth line of the sixth stanza.
10. How might a rich man benefit your town or city by charity?
11. Would the giving of a playground or park be charity?
12. Which is better charity, to give a poor man a sum of money or to give him an opportunity to work at good wages? If you were poor, which would you prefer?

LESSON 190

SELECTION TO BE MEMORIZED

Thank God every morning when you get up, that you have something to do that day which must be done whether you like it or not. Being forced to work, and forced to do your best, will breed in you a hundred virtues which the idle never knew.

—CHARLES KINGSLEY

1. Which people do you think are happier, those who have regular work to do, or those who spend their time in pleasure? Think of someone who seems to be very happy. Why is he happy? Do you think the very rich are any happier than other people?
2. Memorize the paragraph by Charles Kingsley.
3. Write the paragraph from memory.

LESSON 191

COMPOSITION

1. Write a composition, stating what characteristics you like in a boy or girl, and what traits you do not like.

In your composition you may refer to—
A. Qualities of mind
B. Disposition
C. Habits
D. Personal appearance, including neatness

LESSON 192

QUOTATIONS

1. Bring to class quotations and stories to illustrate the following topics: *politeness, industry, truthfulness, kindness to animals.*

LESSON 193

SELECTION TO BE MEMORIZED

TODAY

So here hath been dawning
Another blue Day;
Think, wilt thou let it
Slip useless away?

Out of Eternity
This new Day is born;
Into Eternity,
At night, will return.

Behold it aforetime
　　No eye ever did;
So soon it forever
　　From all eyes is hid.

Here hath been dawning
　　Another blue Day;
Think, wilt thou let it
　　Slip useless away?

　　　　　　　　—THOMAS CARLYLE

1. What lesson do you think the author meant that this poem should teach?
2. What do you understand by a "useless" day? How might such a day have been spent?
3. Use in sentences:
   A. eternity B. aforetime C. behold D. dawning
4. Memorize the poem.

LESSON 194

COMPOSITION

1. Write a composition with two parts. In Part One, tell how a boy or girl let a day "slip useless away."
2. In Part Two, tell how a boy or girl did not let the day "slip useless away."

LESSON 195

SUMMARY—Continued from Lesson 150

TO REMEMBER

When you speak of yourself and one or more others, mention yourself last.

Words that have the same or nearly the same meaning are called *synonyms*.

When animals or objects talk and act like people, they are said to be *personified*.

The name of a person or object personified usually begins with a capital letter.

A sentence that asks a question is called an *interrogative* sentence.

A sentence that commands or requests is called an *imperative* sentence.

A sentence that exclaims, or is introduced by *what* or *how* (not asking questions), is called an *exclamatory* sentence.

A sentence that states something is called a *declarative* sentence.

Titles of poems, books, etc., when used in sentences, are either italicized or enclosed in quotation marks.

PART THREE
LESSON 196

A STORY ABOUT GEORGE WASHINGTON

The character of a great and good man may often be seen in acts that are of an everyday kind. For example, you may get a glimpse of George Washington from a little incident, which, we may be sure, taught a corporal in the Continental army to know him better than ever before.

Early one morning Washington went alone to see for himself what his soldiers were doing in a camp which he had ordered to be fortified. The weather was so cold that he wore a long overcoat with a great cape. The coat hid his uniform, and his hat and cape did not leave much of his face to be seen. For this reason, the soldiers who saw him did not know that the tall man passing by was their great general, George Washington.

At one point in his walk he came upon a few men

who, under the command of a corporal, were building a breastwork of logs. The soldiers were bending over a very heavy log, and were just about to raise it to the top of the breastwork, when General Washington came walking by.

The corporal stood at one side giving orders. "Heave ho!" he cried. "All together! Up with it! Now!" The men lifted with all their might until the log was almost in its place; but they could not raise it quite high enough.

The corporal shouted again, "Heave! Up with it! Up! Up!" but he did not put his hand to it himself. The men struggled and strained; but they had done their best and the heavy log was about to sink back into their arms.

At this moment Washington ran to them, and with his great strength gave them the needed help. The log was quickly lifted upon the breastwork and rolled into place. The grateful men thanked the stranger, but the corporal paid no attention to him.

Then Washington turned to him and said in a stern voice: "Why don't you help your men with this heavy lifting?"

"Why don't I?" said the man. "Don't you see that I am a corporal?"

"Indeed!" replied Washington, as he unbuttoned his coat and showed his uniform. "Well, I am the commander in chief! The next time you have a log too heavy for your men to lift, send for me." Then turning upon his heel, he walked away.

We may be sure that the corporal learned a lesson that many men need to learn, and that the soldiers came to know their great general better than they had ever known him before.

1. What lesson do you think the author meant that this story should teach?

2. Read the lines that show General Washington was ready to help his men and share their hardships.

3. What do you think must have been the feelings of the soldiers that General Washington helped?

4. What good qualities did General Washington show?

5. Why did the corporal not help the soldiers?

6. Make an outline of this story.

7. Tell the story from your outline.

LESSON 197

SUBJECT AND PREDICATE

A. The moon is very beautiful.

B. Its soft yellow light brightens the earth.

1. What object is spoken about in the first sentence?

Note: The *moon* is called the *subject* of the sentence.

The part of a sentence that names that about which something is said is the *subject*.

2. What is said about the moon?

Note: What is said about the moon, *is very beautiful*, is called the *predicate* of the sentence. The part of the sentence that says something about the object named by the subject is the *predicate*.

3. What is spoken about in the second sentence?

4. What is said about *its soft yellow light?*

5. What is the subject, and what is the predicate of the second sentence?

6. Write sentences, using the following as subjects:

A. The Panama Canal

B. A range of high mountains

C. The governor of our state

D. The great Mississippi River

7. Write sentences, using the following as predicates:

A. is the largest state in the Union

B. spins a web from which silk is made

C. is made from the sap of a tree

LESSON 198

SELECTION FOR STUDY

October! Orchard of the year! Ripened seeds shake in their pods. Apples drop in the stillest hours. Leaves begin to let go when no wind is out, and swing in long waverings to the earth, which they touch without sound, and lie looking up, till winds rake them, and heap them in fence corners. The woods are thinner, so that we can see the heavens plainer. The days are calm. The nights are tranquil. The year's work is done. She walks in gorgeous apparel, looking upon her long labor, and her serene eye sayeth, "It is good."

—HENRY WARD BEECHER

1. Compare this paragraph with "October's Bright Blue Weather," Lesson 124. Find references in the poem similar to those in the paragraph.

2. Expain: "swing in long waverings," "the winds rake them," "are tranquil," "gorgeous apparel."

3. Write the quotation from dictation.

LESSON 199

REVIEW

1. Complete the following sentences by referring to the quotation from Henry Ward Beecher in Lesson 198:

   A. There is an exclamation point after *October*, because _____.

   B. There is a period after *pods*, because _____.

   C. There are an apostrophe and *s* after year, because _____.

   D. There is a comma after *sayeth*, because _____.

   E. There are quotation marks around *it is good*, because _____.

   F. *It* begins with a capital letter, because _____.

1. Copy the following sentences, and draw a line under the subject of each:

   A. Ripened seeds shake in their pods.

   B. Apples drop in the stillest hours.

   C. Leaves fall to the ground.

   D. The days are calm.

   E. The nights are tranquil.

   F. The year's work is done.

   G. She walks in gorgeous apparel.

3. Draw two lines under the predicate of each sentence.

LESSON 200

SELECTION TO BE MEMORIZED

A haze on the far horizon,
The infinite, tender sky,
The rich, ripe tint of the cornfields,
And the wild geese sailing high—
And all over upland and lowland
The charm of the goldenrod—
Some of us call it autumn,
And others call it God.

—WILLIAM HERBERT CARRUTH

1. What colors would be used in painting the picture suggested by this poem? Describe the picture.
2. Memorize the poem.
3. Write the poem from memory.

LESSON 201

LETTER WRITING

1. Write a letter asking a friend to take dinner with you and go for a ride next Saturday. State at what time you will have dinner, and when you expect to return from the ride.
2. Write a letter answering the invitation. If it is impossible to accept, state why.

THE GLEANERS

From a painting by Millet

LESSON 202

PICTURE STUDY—THE GLEANERS

The Gleaners was painted by Jean Francois Millet (pronounced mē-ɛlā), an artist who loved the peasant people of France.

1. The picture shows a broad wheat field where there has been a plentiful harvest. Three women have come to the field to pick up the stray pieces of wheat that the reapers have left. The artist has tried to portray the pathos of the poor peasant woman's life of toil and privation. Has he succeeded in his attempt?

2. What colors do you think the artist used in painting the picture?

3. Notice that the figures of the women seem to stand out from the page. This effect was obtained by the skillful use of light and shade. Find the places where the light is strongest and where the shade is heaviest.

4. Describe the background of the picture. In what ways does it suggest that the owner of the field was a man of wealth?

5. What part of the picture suggests poverty?

6. Does the picture make you feel sad, or glad?

LESSON 203

COMPOUND SUBJECT AND PREDICATE

A. Men and women work in the fields, in France.
B. The reapers cut the grain and carry it to the barn.

1. The first sentence has two subjects; name them.
2. What is the predicate of the first sentence?
3. What is the subject of the second sentence?
4. Name the two predicates in the second sentence.
Note: **When two or more simple subjects are united they form a** *compound subject.*
Note: **When two or more simple predicates are united they form a** *compound predicate.*
5. Name the subjects and predicates in the following sentences and tell which are compound:
   A. Bushes and trees were covered with soft, white snow.
   B. Apples, peaches, and pears grew in the orchard.
   C. The farmer plowed the ground and planted the seed.
   D. The great trees and the sparkling brooks made the meadow beautiful.

E. New York and Chicago are large cities.
F. The women gathered the grain and ground it into flour.
G. The rain watered the thirsty fields and made them fresh and green again.
H. Millet and Corot were great artists.
I. The leaves let go of the branches and floated gently to the earth.
J. History and geography are very interesting studies.

LESSON 204

SELECTION FOR STUDY

JULY

When the scarlet cardinal tells
  Her dream to the dragonfly,
And the lazy breeze makes a nest in the trees,
  And murmurs a lullaby,
    It is July.
When tangled cobweb pulls
  The cornflower's cap awry,
And the lilies tall lean over the wall
  To bow to the butterfly,
    It is July.

When the heat like a mist veil floats,
And poppies flame in the rye,
And the silver note in the streamlet's throat
Has softened almost to a sigh,
It is July.

When the hours are so still that time
Forgets them, and lets them lie
'Neath petals pink till the night stars wink
At the sunset in the sky,
It is July.

When each finger-post by the way
Says that Slumbertown is nigh;
When the grass is tall, and the roses fall,
And nobody wonders why,
It is July.

—Susan Hartley Swett

1. What is meant by the first and second lines of the first stanza?
2. How could the cobweb pull "the cornflower's cap awry?"
3. Why is the word "flame" used in the third stanza?
4. Explain lines three and four of the third stanza.
5. How many pictures do you find in this poem?
6. Which part do you like best?
7. Memorize the two stanzas that mean the most to you.

LESSON 205

TRANSPOSED ORDER

A. The ripe nuts fall to the ground.
B. To the ground fall the ripe nuts.

1. What is the subject of the first sentence? (Notice that in the second sentence the subject is placed after the predicate.)

Note: **When the subject of a sentence is placed after the predicate, the sentence is said to be in** *transposed order.*

2. Name the subject in each of the following sentences; then reconstruct the sentence, placing the subject before the predicate:

A. In the tranquil waters of the lake are reflected a few late flowers.
B. Calm and quiet are the days.
C. In their pods shake the ripened seeds.
D. Through the leafless branches may be seen the stars.
E. Finished is the work of the year.
F. So still are the hours that time forgets them.
G. On the far horizon is a faint haze.
H. Over upland and lowland grows the goldenrod.
I. Near the waterfall stands an old mill.

3. Name the subject in each of the following sentences; then reconstruct the sentence, placing the subject after the predicate:

A. Lilies tall lean over the wall.
B. Poppies flame in the rye.
C. The little birds have flown from the nest.
D. The heat floats like a mist.
E. The streamlet's music is like a sigh.

Note: It is often best to rearrange the words of the predicate when reconstructing a sentence.

LESSON 206

CONVERSATION—THE SCHOOL

Talk about the following:

1. The number of school buildings in your city, town, or district.
2. How are schools supported?
3. Expense of maintaining schools.
4. What are the duties of the board of education?
5. Has your state a compulsory school law?
6. What are the advantages of such a law?
7. What higher schools or colleges are near you?
8. Where is your state university?
9. Tell what you can about the state university.

LESSON 207

DEBATE

A boy or girl who has received a high school education is better fitted for business life than the pupil who goes to work after completing only the elementary course.

1. Debate the subject. Read suggestions regarding a debate, Lesson 108.

LESSON 208

SELECTION FOR STUDY

THE INVENTION OF PRINTING

Seven hundred years ago, every book was written by hand, for the art of printing was then unknown. If there were pictures, they were drawn with a pen or painted with a brush. It required a great deal of labor and time to make a book, and when one was finished it was so costly that only a very rich person could afford to own it.

There were no bookstores such as we have now, and books were very few. But in the great schools and large monasteries there were men called copyists, whose business it was to make written copies of such works as were in demand. There were other men called illuminators, who ornamented the books with beautiful initials and chapter headings, and sometimes encircled the pages with borders made with ink of different colors.

At last some copyist who had several copies to make of the same book thought of a new plan. He carved a copy of each page on a block of wood. If there was to be a picture, he carved that too, much in the same way that wood carvings are made now. When the book was finished, it was carefully wet with a thin, inky substance; then a sheet of paper was laid upon it and pressed down until an impression of the carved block was printed. Each page was treated in the same way, but the paper could be printed only on one side. When all was finished, the leaves were stitched together and made into a book. It was not so handsome a book as those written with pen and ink; but after the block had once been engraved, the copyist could make fifty copies of it in less time than he could make one copy by hand.

TOPICS FOR CONVERSATION

1. Tell what you can of the way in which books were made, before the invention of printing.
2. Compare the opportunities for education that people have now, with those that people had seven hundred years ago.
3. Tell what you can of typesetting and modern methods of printing.

LESSON 209

COMPOSITION

1. Clip news items from papers. Read to the class those which you think are best. Observe the form in which they are written.
2. Write local news items suggested by events of the past week. Let each item contain words enough for ten or more printed lines.
3. Write an item for a newspaper, on one of the following subjects:
   A. Need of a new schoolhouse
   B. Damage done by storm
   C. The baseball game
   D. The act of a brave boy
   E. Increase in shipments of fruit
   F. The automobile races
   G. The water supply inadequate
   H. Great fire in the business section
   I. Need of rain
   J. Frost in the south, the orange crop injured
   K. Suffering among the poor caused by the continued cold
   L. A distinguished visitor; his comments on local conditions

LESSON 210

DICTATION

Wherever a ship plows the sea, or a plow furrows the field; wherever a mine yields its treasure; wherever a ship or a railroad train carries freight to market; wherever the smoke of a furnace rises, or the clang of the loom resounds; even in the lonely garret where the seamstress plies her busy needle—there is industry.

—JAMES A. GARFIELD

Note: *Ship* **is the name of something that sails upon the sea.**

Note: *Sea* **is the name of a great body of water.**

1. How many other names can you find in the paragraph?

Note: All words used as names are called *nouns*.

2. Make a list of the nouns in the paragraph.
3. Write the paragraph from dictation.

LESSON 211

NOUNS

1. Write five nouns that are names of objects at your home.
2. Write five nouns that are names of objects you saw on the way to school.

3. Write five nouns that are names of articles of food.
4. Write five nouns that are names of musical instruments.
5. Write three nouns that are names of materials used for clothing.
6. Write three nouns that are names of parts of a wagon, motorcycle, or automobile.
7. Write five nouns that are names of parts of the human body.
8. Write five nouns that are names of flowers.

LESSON 212

SELECTION FOR STUDY

THE MUSIC OF LABOR

The banging of the hammer,
The whirling of the plane,
The crashing of the busy saw,
The creaking of the crane,
The ringing of the anvil,
The grating of the drill,
The clattering of the turning lathe,
The whirling of the mill,
The buzzing of the spindle,
The rattling of the loom,
The puffing of the engine,

The fan's continual boom,
The clipping of the tailor's shears.
The driving of the awl—
These sounds of honest industry
I love—I love them all!
The clinking of the magic type,
The earnest talk of men,
The toiling of the giant press,
The scratching of the pen,
The bustling of the market man
As he hies him to the town,
The halloo from the tree top
As the ripened fruit comes down,
The busy sound of thrashers
As they cleave the ripened grain,
The husker's joke and catch of glee
'Neath the moonlight on the plain,
The kind voice of the dairyman,
The shepherd's gentle call—
These sounds of honest industry
I love—I love them all.

1. Read the lines that refer to the work of the tailor, the shoemaker, the author, the farmer, the engineer, the weaver, the blacksmith, the carpenter.
2. Which industry referred to in this lesson do you know most about? Tell what you can about it.

LESSON 213

MICHAEL ANGELO

More than five hundred years ago, Michael Angelo, one of the greatest artists the world has ever known, lived in Italy. He not only painted beautiful pictures, but he made plans for magnificent buildings and he chiseled splendid pieces of sculpture. The following story is told about one of his greatest statues:

In Florence, near the gate of the city, there was a huge block of marble; because of its great size no sculptor or builder had tried to use it, so it had become covered with rubbish and was almost forgotten.

One day, as Michael Angelo was passing through the city, he saw the great block, and brushing away the dirt that almost hid it he saw with surprise that it was of the whitest marble. As he gazed at it he longed to change the great stone into a statue that should be more splendid than anything he had yet made.

With mallet and chisel he began to work. Weeks went by and the ground all about became covered with small pieces of marble.

Months passed, and still Michael Angelo, with greatest care, cut away, bit by bit, the tiny pieces. If the mallet should slip, if the chisel should cut too deep, the statue might be ruined; but the hand of the sculptor was sure, and after eighteen months of careful, patient work the artist laid aside his tools.

From the statue by Michael Angelo
THE HEAD OF DAVID

Instead of the great shapeless block, too large and too clumsy to be of use, there stood the beautiful statue of David the Shepherd Boy.

The people were delighted with the wonderful piece of work; they placed it at the main entrance to the city, where it stood for centuries. The people of Florence thought that no harm could come to them while David stood at the gate.

1. Why did the block of marble mean more to Michael Angelo than it did to other people?
2. What sort of mental picture do you think he had as he gazed at the block?
3. Tell the story of the making of the statue.
4. Tell the story of David the Shepherd Boy, as it is told in the Bible.

LESSON 214

PRONOUNS

1. In the first paragraph of Lesson 213 who is meant by *he*? To whom does the word *his* refer?
2. In the second paragraph to whom does *it* refer? In the fourth paragraph *him* is used instead of what word? For what word is *they* used?
3. In the fifth paragraph *his* is used instead of what word?

Note: A word that is used in place of a noun is called a *pronoun.*

Note: The noun for which a pronoun stands is called its *antecedent.*

5. Copy the pronouns in Lesson 198.
6. Write after each pronoun its antecedent.

LESSON 215

COMPOSITION—DESCRIPTION OF A PLACE

Travelers going to a strange city find of great service a guidebook containing the names and short descriptions of the principal places of interest.

1. Write a travelers' guide for the place in which you live.
2. If you live in the city, write of the buildings, stores, parks, etc., that would be of interest to visitors.
3. Give a short description of each of the more important.
4. If you live in a small town, write of the surroundings, the places of natural beauty, fine farms, or any local industry that would interest a visitor.

LESSON 216

COMMON AND PROPER NOUNS

In Florence, near the gate of the city, there was a huge block of pure white marble.

1. Name the nouns in this sentence.
2. Does *block* refer to any particular object, or to one of a class of objects?
3. Does *Florence* refer to a particular place, or to one of a class of places?

Note: A noun that refers to a particular person, place, or object is called a *proper noun*. *Florence* is a proper noun.

Note: A noun that belongs to one of a class of persons, places, or objects is called a *common noun*. *Block* is a common noun.

4. With what kind of letter do all proper nouns begin?
5. Write the names of five cities.
6. Write the names of five states.
7. Write the names of five countries.
8. Write the names of five rivers.
9. Write the names of five great men.

LESSON 217

SELECTION FOR STUDY

DOWN TO SLEEP

November woods are bare and still;
November days are clear and bright;
Each noon burns up the morning chill;
The morning's snow is gone by night.
Each day my steps grow slow, grow light,
As through the woods I reverent creep,
Watching all things lie "down to sleep."

I never knew before what beds,
Fragrant to smell and soft to touch,
The forest sifts and shapes and spreads.
I never knew before how much
Of human sound there is in such
Low tones as through the forest sweep.

Each day I find new coverlids
Tucked in, and more sweet eyes shut tight;
Sometimes the viewless mother bids
Her ferns kneel down, full in my sight;
I hear their chorus of "good-night";
And half I smile and half I weep,
Listening while they lie "down to sleep."

—HELEN HUNT JACKSON

1. What is meant by the third line of the first stanza?
2. Why does the author use the word "reverent," in the sixth line?
3. What words describe "November woods?"
4. What words describe "November days?"
5. How does the forest "spread beds?"
6. Explain lines one and two of the third stanza.
7. Who is meant by the "viewless mother?"
8. From what are the words "down to sleep" quoted?
9. Describe a picture that might illustrate this poem.
10. Who wrote this poem?
11. Find in this book "October's Bright Blue Weather." Compare it with this poem. Which has the prettier word pictures?
12. Read again the quotation from Henry Ward Beecher, Lesson 198. Compare it with this poem. Do you find similar ideas in the two?

LESSON 218

COMPOSITION—A LOST ARTICLE

When an article is lost, the owner often places a notice in the paper; such a notice should describe the lost article in as few words as possible.

Lost, between the courthouse and the post office, a black silk umbrella; handle of gold, with initials E. G. C. Reward offered for its return to Edwin G. Curtis, 642 Linn St.

1. Using this as a model, write a notice regarding a lost article.

LESSON 219

POSSESSIVES

A. The morning's snow is gone by night.
B. The stars are the night's candles.
C. The sculptor's chisel cut the block of marble.
D. Sculptors' chisels are sharp.
E. The artist's greatest picture was not sold.
F. Artists' materials are sold at this store.

1. Copy from the sentences all nouns in the possessive form. Which are in the possessive singular? Which are in the possessive plural?
2. Write the possessive singular of each of the following nouns:

A. day	E. forest	I. river
B. bed	F. oak	J. robin
C. rose	G. town	K. maple
D. oriole	H. village	L. winter

3. Write the possessive plural of each of the nouns.
4. How is the possessive of nouns in the singular formed?
5. How is the possessive of nouns in the plural ending in *s* formed?
6. Write six nouns whose plural forms do not end in *s*.

Note: The possessive plural of such nouns is formed by adding the apostrophe and *s* to the plural form.

7. Form the possessive plurals of the nouns you have written.

LESSON 220

CONVERSATION—COAL

1. What sections of the United States produce much coal?
2. Tell what you can of the way in which coal is mined.
3. Tell uses of coal for transportation, manufacturing, heating, etc.
4. What is the difference between soft coal, anthracite, and semi-anthracite? (Bring specimens.)
5. Compare coal and wood as to value for fuel.

LESSON 221

COMPOSITION

1. Write a composition on coal. Include the points discussed in Lesson 220.

LESSON 222

CONVERSATION—ELECTRICITY

1. Tell what you can of the way in which houses are lighted by electricity.
2. Compare electric lights with other means of lighting.
3. How does electricity enable us to talk long distances?
4. What machines are run by electricity?
5. How does electricity aid in transportation?
6. Find out what you can about one of the following, and be prepared to tell the rest of the class about it:

   A. airplanes   D. motor boats
   B. motor cars   E. telephones
   C. motorcycles   F. radios

THE FIRST RAILWAY TRAIN

LESSON 223

PICTURE STUDY AND LETTER

1. Tell what you see in the picture.
2. Describe the engine and coaches.
3. What is the power that moves the train?
4. How is that power generated? How is it controlled?
5. Describe a modern engine and compare it with this one.
6. Imagine yourself one of the persons who went to see the first railway train, and write a letter to a cousin describing the wonderful event. Tell your impression when you first saw the engine and of your wonder when it began to move.

LESSON 224

CONVERSATION—TRANSPORTATION

1. Talk about the various means of transportation. When and where was the prairie schooner used?

2. Where are dogs and sleds used?
3. Where are camels used?
4. What advantages have camels over horses, for the kind of work they have to do?

5. Tell what you can about sailboats.
6. In what respects is the steamboat an improvement over a sailboat?
7. Tell what you can of the equipment of a modern passenger train.

8. Bring pictures showing various means of transportation.

9. Write a description of one of the following:

A. a sailboat
D. a street car
B. an ocean steamer
E. an automobile
C. a passenger train
F. a motor cycle

LESSON 225

DEBATE

Resolved, that the study of geography is of more value to the pupil than arithmetic.

1. Debate this subject. For suggestions regarding a debate see Lesson 108.

LESSON 226

DICTATION—TRANSPORTATION

Goods are transported not only on railroads and ocean ships, but also by trucks on roads and by boats on rivers and canals. Trucks are often used to transport goods to market or to the railroad or boat, but it is a more expensive mode of transportation. The most expensive mode of transportation is by airplane, but it is the fastest. Transportation by boats on rivers and canals and by freighters and tankers on the ocean is comparatively cheap, although much slower than by railroad or truck, and it is much used, especially for heavy and bulky articles.

1. Write the paragraph from dictation.
2. Copy fifteen nouns from the paragraph; place the singular nouns in one list and the plural nouns in another.
3. What pronoun do you find? State its antecedent each time that it is used.
4. Use the following words in sentences:

    A. transported   D. canal
    B. comparatively   E. especially
    C. bulky   F. distance

LESSON 227

CONVERSATION—GOOD ROADS

1. Where are the best roads in your neighbor-hood?
2. How were they made?
3. What materials are best for country roads?
4. How are town or city roads paved?
5. How should a road be graded?
6. Of what advantage to the farmer are good roads?

LESSON 228

RAILROADS

1. Tell the names of all the railroads you know.
2. What line, or lines, would you take to go from your home to one of the following places: New York, Chicago, Denver, San Francisco, Minneapolis, Kansas City, New Orleans, Cincinnati?
3. Plan trips to one or more of the following places: Yellow Stone National Park; Washington, D. C.; Florida; Colorado; Yosemite Valley; Grand Canyon, AZ; Niagara Falls; California.
4. Which of these places would you most like to visit?

THE BREAKING WAVE

5. At what time of year would your trip be most pleasant?
6. What places of interest would you like to visit on the way?
7. Bring to class descriptions and pictures of interesting places you would like to visit, or find poems describing any of the places.

LESSON 229

PICTURE STUDY—THE BREAKING WAVE

1. Study this picture. What does it suggest to you?
2. What other name might the painter have given to the picture?
3. Have you seen a storm on the ocean or on a large lake? Tell about it if you have.
4. Why does the artist show so much of the sea and so little of the sky? Find another picture where the opposite is true.
5. Compare this picture with the *Return of the Fishing Boats*, page 103. Which picture do you like better?
6. What colors do you think were used in painting this picture?
7. Can you find any poem or description suggested by the picture?

LESSON 230

ADVERTISEMENT AND ANSWER

Bookkeeper wanted, for real estate office; chance for promotion. State experience and salary desired. Best of references required. D 643, Times.

1. Write a letter which might be sent in answer to this advertisement. The letter should be sent to D 643, Times Office.

LESSON 231

WRITING ADVERTISEMENTS

1. Bring advertisements clipped from newspapers.
2. Study them and select the ones you consider the best.
3. Write an advertisement of not more than thirty words for each of the following:
   A. To Rent—Furnished Room
   B. For Sale—House
   C. Wanted to Purchase—Pony
   D. Situation Wanted—Stenographer
   E. Lost—Dog
   F. Wanted to Rent—House
   G. Found—Pocketbook

LESSON 232

SELECTION FOR STUDY

THE BLUE JAY

O Blue Jay up in the maple tree,
Shaking your throat with such bursts of glee,
　　How did you happen to be so blue?
Did you steal a bit of the lake for your crest,
And fasten blue violets into your vest?
　　Tell me, I pray you—tell me true!

Did you dip your wings in azure dye,
When April began to paint the sky,
　　That was pale with the winter's stay?
Or were you hatched from a bluebell bright,
'Neath the warm, gold breast of a sunbeam light,
　　By the river one blue spring day?

O Blue Jay up in the maple tree,
A-tossing your saucy head at me,
　　With ne'er a word for my questioning,
Pray, cease for a moment your "ting-a-link,"
And hear when I tell you what I think,
　　You bonniest bit of the spring.

I think when the Lord God made the flowers,
To grow in these mossy fields of ours,
　　Periwinkles and violets rare,

There was left of the spring's own color, blue,
Plenty to fashion a flower whose hue
  Would be richer than all and as fair.

So, God in his majestic way,
Made one great blossom so bright and gay,
  The lily beside it seemed blurred;
And then he said, "We will toss it in air;
So many blue blossoms grow everywhere,
  Let this pretty one be a bird!"

  —SUSAN HARTLEY SWETT (ADAPTATION)

1. Explain: "azure," "dye," "bonniest."
2. What is meant by the second and third lines of the second stanza?
3. State in your own words the thought of the author concerning the making of the blue jay.

LESSON 233

CONVERSATION—BIRDS' NESTS

Every kind of bird makes its own kind of nest. Some nests are placed on the ground, some are built in the tops of high trees, and some in low bushes. Some nests are made of mud and soft grass, some are of hay and hair, and some are constructed of a few branches laid carelessly together on the ground.

1. Find out about the nests of as many of the following birds as you can:

A. robin   E. sparrow   I. duck   M. eagle
B. cowbird   F. blue jay   J. crow   N. flicker,
C. wren   G. catbird   K. hawk   O. swan
D. heron   H. shrike   L. owl   P. blackbird
   Q. mocking bird   T. barn swallow
   R. chimney swallow   U. cliff swallow
   S. Baltimore oriole   V. goldfinch

2. How many of these birds can you recognize when you see them?

LESSON 234

DICTATION

THE ORIOLE'S NEST

When the orchards are in bloom, the oriole returns from the south, and with his mate begins the construction of a wonderful home. The place chosen is usually the top of some high tree, and there the birds hang their pocket-shaped nest. The top is fastened to a forked twig at the fork, in order that the door shall be kept open. The pocket often hangs free, but sometimes the bottom is fastened to near-by twigs by strong hairs or strings. The framework of the nest is made of twine or long horsehairs, through which the oriole weaves fine grass, hair, and bits of wood fiber.

1. Find in this paragraph a compound word.
2. Find a sentence containing a series of words.
3. How is the sentence punctuated?
4. Write the paragraph from dictation.

LESSON 235

BIOGRAPHY OF AN ORIOLE

1. Tell of—
A. Its early home
B. Learning to fly
C. Learning to sing
D. How it spent the summer
E. Its flight south
F. The difference between north and south
G. The winter in the south
H. The return to the north
I. Try to include some adventure that might happen to a bird—perhaps it was almost caught by a hawk, a cat, or a big snake.

A WINTER SCENE

LESSON 236

SELECTION FOR STUDY

WINTER

The wind sweeps through the forest with a sound like the blast of a trumpet. The dry leaves whirl in eddies through the air. A fretwork of hoarfrost covers the plain. The stagnant water in the pools and ditches is frozen into fantastic figures. Nature ceases from her labors and prepares for the great change. In the low-hanging clouds, the sharp air, like a busy shuttle, weaves her shroud of snow. There is a melancholy and continual roar in the tops of the tall pines, like the roar of a cataract. It is the funeral anthem of the dying year.

—HENRY W. LONGFELLOW

1. Why is the wind compared to the "blast of a trumpet"?
2. In what ways does Nature prepare "for the great change"?
3. Explain "Nature ceases from her labors."
4. Describe the picture that this paragraph suggests.
5. What word describes "leaves"?
6. What word describes "water"?
7. What word describes "figures"?
8. Find other words in this paragraph that describe.
Note: A word that describes a noun or pronoun is called an *adjective*.
9. Write the paragraph from dictation.

LESSON 237

CONVERSATION

1. Discuss the following sentences in class; tell what you think each means and if possible illustrate with some short story:

A. Wealth cannot buy health.

B. Evil news rides fast.

C. Every cloud has a silver lining.

D. A good name is rather to be chosen than great riches.

E. A soft answer turneth away wrath.

LESSON 238

DICTATION

The Bells

Hear the sledges with the bells—
Silver bells!
What a world of merriment their melody foretells!
How they tinkle, tinkle, tinkle,
In the icy air of night!
While the stars that oversprinkle
All the heavens, seem to twinkle
With a crystalline delight;
Keeping time, time, time,
In a sort of Runic rhyme,
To the tintinnabulation that so musically wells
From the bells, bells, bells, bells,
Bells, bells, bells—
From the jingling and the tinkling of the bells.

—Edgar Allan Poe

1. In this poem the author tried to reproduce in verse the music made by sleigh bells.
2. Memorize the poem.
3. Write the poem either from memory or from dictation.

LESSON 239

COMPOSITION

1. If you had been given a large sum of money to spend for improvements in your neighborhood, tell what you would do.
2. If roads or bridges need repairing, tell how you would have the work done; if public buildings need tearing down, tell which ones, and how you would replace them.

LESSON 240

CHOICE OF ADJECTIVES

1. Copy the following nouns, placing a suitable adjective before each:

A. wind	G. snow	M. mountains	S. fruit
B. forest	H. trees	N. valleys	T. night
C. leaves	I. flowers	O. plains	U. engine
D. water	J. bells	P. river	V. picture
E. clouds	K. waves	Q. ocean	W. story
F. air	L. rocks	R. moon	X. song

LESSON 241

SELECTION FOR STUDY

Did you never, in walking in the fields, come across a large flat stone, which had lain, nobody knows how long, just where you found it, with the grass forming a little hedge, as it were, all around it, close to its edges—and have you in obedience to a kind of feeling that told you it had been lying there long enough, insinuated your stick or your foot or your fingers under its edge and turned it over as a housewife turns a cake, when she says to herself, "It's done brown enough by this time"? What an odd revelation, and what an unforeseen and unpleasant surprise to a small community, the very existence of which you had not suspected, until the sudden dismay and scattering among its members produced by your turning the old stone over! Blades of grass flattened down, colorless, matted together, as if they had been bleached and ironed; hideous crawling creatures; black, glossy crickets, with their long filaments sticking out like the whips of four-horse stagecoaches; motionless slug-like creatures, young larvæ, perhaps more horrible in their pulpy stillness than even in the infernal wiggle of maturity! But no sooner is the stone turned and the wholesome light of day let upon this compressed and blinded community of creeping things, than all of them which enjoy the luxury of legs—and some of them have a good many—rush round wildly, butting each other and everything in their way, and end in a general stampede for underground retreats from the region poisoned by sunshine. *Next year* you will find the grass growing tall and green where the stone lay; the ground bird builds her nest where the beetle had his hole; the dandelion and the buttercup are growing there, and the broad fans of insect-angels open and shut over their golden disks.

—OLIVER WENDELL HOLMES

1. Find the meanings of these words:
   A. revelation   C. unforeseen   E. community
   B. existence   D. larvæ   F. compressed
2. Use the words in sentences.
3. What is meant by "insect-angels"?
4. To what does "their golden disks" refer?
5. How do you explain the expression, "poisoned by sunshine"?
6. Did you ever have an experience similar to the one the author describes?
7. From this selection copy—
   A. Ten nouns in the singular
   B. Ten nouns in the plural
   C. Five pronouns and write after each its antecedent
   D. Ten adjectives and write after each the word that it modifies

LESSON 242

COMPOSITION

1. Write a composition on one of the following subjects:
   A. My first ride on horseback
   B. My first ride on a bicycle
   C. My first ride in a rowboat
   D. My first ride in an automobile
   E. My first ride in a motor boat
   State—
      a. When it was
      b. Where you went
      c. With whom you went
      d. Some interesting experience connected with the ride

LESSON 243

DEBATE

More pleasure can be obtained from a horse and carriage than from an automobile.

1. Debate this subject. Read suggestions regarding a debate, Lesson 108.

LESSON 244

PICTURE STUDY—THE HORSE FAIR

Rosa Bonheur was a French artist who loved animals and painted many beautiful pictures of them.

The Horse Fair is the most famous of all her pictures. The artist spent nearly two years in making sketches for this great painting. Her friends in Paris lent her their finest horses that she might draw them, but this was not enough, so she visited horse fairs and horse markets. She made sketches of horses in all sorts of positions, then with these sketches before her she began work on the large picture.

1. Look carefully at the picture; notice the different positions of the horses. Think how many sketches the artist needed.
2. Which horse is the principal one of the picture? Which did you notice first? Is it in the center of the picture? Does an artist ever place the principal subject exactly in the center?
3. Can you name another artist who painted pictures of animals? In what country did he live?

From a painting Rosa Bonheur

THE HORSE FAIR

LESSON 245

SELECTION FOR STUDY

The Horse's Prayer

To you, my Master, I offer my prayer: Feed me, water me, and care for me, and when the day's work is done, provide me with shelter, a clean, dry bed, and a stall wide enough for me to lie down in comfort.

Always be kind to me. Talk to me; your voice often means as much to me as the reins. Pet me sometimes, that I may serve you the more gladly and learn to love you. Do not jerk the reins, and do not whip me when going up hill. Never strike, beat, or kick me when I do not understand what you want, but give me a chance to understand you. Watch me, and if I fail to do your bidding, see if something is not wrong with my harness or my feet.

Do not check me so that I cannot have the free use of my head. If you insist that I wear blinders, so that I cannot see behind me as it was intended I should, I pray you be careful that the blinders stand well out from my eyes.

Do not overload me, or hitch me where water will drip on me. Keep me well shod. Examine my teeth when I do not eat; I may have an ulcerated tooth, and that, you know, is very painful. Do not tie my head in an unnatural position, or take away my best defense against flies by cutting off my tail.

I cannot tell you when I am thirsty, so give me clean, cool water, often. Save me, by all means in your power, from that fatal disease—the glanders. I cannot tell you in words when I am sick, so watch me, that by signs you may know my condition. Give me all possible shelter from the hot sun, and put a blanket on me, not when I am working, but when I am standing in the cold. Never put a frosty bit in my mouth; first warm it by holding it in your hands.

And finally, O my Master, when my useful strength is gone, do not turn me out to starve or freeze, or sell me to some cruel owner, to be slowly tortured and starved to death; but do you, my Master, take my life in the kindest way, and your God will reward you here and hereafter.

—From *Our Dumb Animals*

1. Mention some ways in which a horse should be cared for.
2. Mention some ways in which a horse should not be treated.
3. In this selection find words in series.
4. Give the rule for the punctuation of words in a series.
5. Find the nouns; write the nouns in the singular in one list, those in the plural in another.

6. In the first line the word *petition* might have been used instead of *prayer.*
7. Find words that might have been used instead of the following: *offer, provide, examine, condition, shelter, reward.*
8. In the first line why is there a comma before *my* and one after *Master?*
9. Write the first and second paragraphs from dictation.

LESSON 246

COMPOSITION

1. Read again "The Horse's Prayer," Lesson 245, then write a dog's prayer. Let your composition tell of ways in which dogs are sometimes neglected or abused.

LESSON 247

ADJECTIVES AND NOUNS

1. Copy the following adjectives, and write after each a suitable noun:

A. transparent	I. porous	Q. smooth
B. downy	J. sticky	R. fleecy
C. slippery	K. brittle	S. acid
D. bitter	L. fragrant	T. grand
E. crisp	M. juicy	U. delicious
F. spacious	N. delicate	V. hug
G. extensive	O. slender	W. indelible
H. nutritious	P. industrious	X. stiff

LESSON 248

SUMMARY—Continued from Lesson 195

To Remember

The part of a sentence that names that about which something is said is the *subject*.

The part of the sentence that says something about the object named by the subject is the *predicate*.

When two or more subjects are united, they form a *compound subject*.

When two or more predicates are united, they form a *compound predicate*.

All words used as names are *nouns*.

A word that is used for a noun is a *pronoun*.

The noun for which a pronoun stands is called its *antecedent*.

A name that belongs to a particular person, place, or object is a *proper noun*.

A name that belongs to any one of a class of persons, places, or objects is a *common noun*.

A proper noun begins with a capital letter.

A word that describes a noun or pronoun is an *adjective*.

Singular nouns form their possessive by adding the apostrophe and *s*.

Plural nouns ending in *s* form their possessive by adding the apostrophe after the *s*.

LESSON 249

SELECTION FOR STUDY

LANDING OF THE PILGRIM FATHERS

The breaking waves dashed high
    On a stern and rock-bound coast,
And the woods against a stormy sky
    Their giant branches tossed;

And the heavy night hung dark
    The hills and waters o'er,
When a band of exiles moored their bark
    On the wild New England shore.

Not as the conqueror comes,
    They, the true-hearted, came;
Not with the roll of the stirring drums,
    And the trumpet that sings of fame;

Not as the flying come,
    In silence and in fear—
They shook the depths of the desert gloom
    With their hymns of lofty cheer.

Amidst the storm they sang,
    And the stars heard and the sea;
And the sounding aisles of the dim woods rang
    To the anthem of the free.

The ocean eagle soared
   From his nest by the white wave's foam,
And the rocking pines of the forest roared—
   This was their welcome home.

There were men with hoary hair
   Amidst that pilgrim band;
Why had they come to wither there,
   Away from their childhood's land?

There was woman's fearless eye,
   Lit by her deep love's truth;
There was manhood's brow serenely high,
   And the fiery heart of youth.

What sought they thus afar?
   Bright jewels of the mine?
The wealth of seas, the spoils of war?
   They sought a faith's pure shrine!

Ay, call it holy ground,
   The soil where first they trod;
They have left unstained what there they found—
   Freedom to worship God.
              —FELICIA D. HEMANS

1. Describe the picture given in the first six lines
of the poem.
2. What do you understand by "rock-bound coast"?

3. What other words might have been used in place of *bark?*
4. Would any other words give the same idea?
5. What does the fifth stanza tell of the character of the people who had come to the new world?
6. What welcome did they receive?
7. Read the lines that describe the different persons in this band of exiles.
8. Why had they come to America?
9. Use in sentences:

A. breaking waves   D. giant branches
B. wild New England shore   E. stormy sky
C. hoary hair   F. dim woods

LESSON 250

SELECTION FOR STUDY

"I shine," says the sun,
"To give the world light,"
"I glimmer," adds the moon,
"To beautify the night."
"I ripple," says the brook,
"I whisper," sighs the breeze,
"I patter," laughs the rain,
"We rustle," call the trees,
"We dance," nod the daisies,
"I twinkle," shines the star,

"We sing," chant the birds,
"How happy we all are!"
"I smile," cries the child,
Gentle, good, and gay;
The sweetest thing of all,
The sunshine of each day.

—LOUISA M. ALCOTT

Note: The word *shine* expresses the action of the sun. *Says* also expresses an action. A word that expresses action is called a *verb*.

1. Copy twelve nouns.
2. Find in the selection divided quotations. How are they punctuated?
3. Copy ten verbs from the selection.
4. Write the selection from dictation.

LESSON 251

VERBS

1. Write a sentence containing—
   A. Five verbs that tell what a horse can do
   B. Three verbs that tell what a dog can do
   C. One verb that tells what the sun does
   D. One verb that tells what the wind does
   E. One verb that tells what the fire does
   F. Three verbs that tell what the bird can do

G. Five verbs that tell what the farmer does.

H. Five verbs that tell what you can do.

2. Copy five verbs from Lesson 236.

LESSON 252

VERBS—Continued

A. In every seed there is a plant.

B. November woods are bare and still.

Note: Some verbs do not express action. In the first sentence we assert no action, but express being.
In the second sentence we express a condition or state of being.
A word that expresses action, being, or state of being is called a *verb*.
Sometimes a verb consists of more than one word; as, *was running, had been running, might have been running*, etc.

1. Copy five verbs from Lesson 198.

2. Copy five verbs from Lesson 204.

3. Copy ten nouns from Lesson 204.

4. Copy nouns, pronouns, adjectives, and verbs from Lesson 208.

LESSON 253
LETTER WRITING

1. Write one of the following:
   A. You have moved, and wish to have the address of a paper or magazine to which you have subscribed changed. Write the letter, giving both the old address and the new.
   B. The pupils in your room wish to use a vacant lot for basketball games. Write a letter to the owner asking permission.
   C. Write a note to your teacher asking if you may be excused from school for part of the day. State why you wish to be absent.

LESSON 254
CONVERSATION

1. Tell what you can of the duties of a judge.
2. Suppose that a man is accused of stealing a sum of money, tell what you can of the manner of conducting the trial.
3. How is the jury chosen? Of how many people is it composed?
4. Who decides whether the accused is guilty?
5. Who pronounces sentence?
6. Explain the terms *attorney for the defense, acquittal.*

LESSON 255

SELECTION FOR STUDY

THE BURIAL OF SIR JOHN MOORE

Not a drum was heard, not a funeral note,
As his corpse to the rampart we hurried;
Not a soldier discharged his farewell shot
O'er the grave where our hero we buried.

We buried him darkly at dead of night,
The sods with our bayonets turning,
By the struggling moonbeam's misty light,
And the lantern dimly burning.

No useless coffin enclosed his breast,
Nor in sheet nor in shroud we wound him;
But he lay like a warrior taking his rest
With his martial cloak around him.

Few and short were the prayers we said,
And we spoke not a word of sorrow;
But we steadfastly gazed on the face of the dead,
And we bitterly thought of the morrow.

We thought as we hollowed his narrow bed
And smoothed down his lonely pillow,
That the foe and the stranger would tread o'er his head,
And we far away on the billow.

Lightly they'll talk of the spirit that's gone,
And o'er his cold ashes upbraid him—
But little he'll reck, if they let him sleep on
In the grave where a Briton has laid him.

But half of our heavy task was done
When the clock struck the hour for retiring;
And we heard the distant and random gun
That the foe was sullenly firing.

Slowly and sadly we laid him down,
From the field of his fame fresh and gory;
We carved not a line, we raised not a stone,
But we left him alone with his glory.

—CHARLES WOLFE

Sir John Moore, a brave English general, was killed in Spain, where the English were fighting against the army of Napoleon. His comrades buried him at night on the battle ground.

1. Why was there no sound of drum or funeral note as the hero was buried?
2. Read the lines that tell the time of the burial.
3. What lines tell of the feeling of the soldiers toward Sir John Moore?
4. Explain the meaning of these words: "rampart," "bayonets," "shroud," "martial," "random."

LESSON 256

CORRECT USE OF WORDS

A. I shall see you soon.

B. This lesson is difficult, but I will learn it.

C. My cousin will see you soon.

D. My cousin shall go to school, even if he does prefer not to go.

1. Which of the sentences express determination?

2. What verb is used with *I*? What verb is used with *my cousin?*

3. Which of the sentences state that something will occur in the future? What verb is used with *I*? What verb is used with *my cousin*?

Note: To express simple future use *shall* with *I* and *we*, use *will* with all other words.
To express determination use *will* with *I* and *we*, use *shall* with all other words.

4. Use *shall* and *will* in sentences expressing simple future, showing that—

A. You expect to go away this summer.

B. Your mother expects to go with you.

C. You both expect to see many strange sights.

D. Your father expects to be with you part of the time.

E. You expect to send post cards to many of your friends.

F. You expect to return before school begins in the fall.

5. Fill each of the following blanks with *shall* or *will*, so that the sentences shall express determination:

A. I _____ finish this work.

B. My dog _____ learn this trick.

C. You _____ not hurt this boy.

D. I _____ tell the truth.

E. You _____ give me my book.

F. We _____ go even if it does rain.

LESSON 257

COMPOSITION—A DESCRIPTION

1. Write a description of the prettiest spot near your home. It may be some place on a river or stream, it may be a part of a park, or a shady nook in the woods. Describe the place, tell how to reach it, and state what there is that makes it especially beautiful.

LESSON 258

SELECTION FOR STUDY

THE SEASONS

As early as the first of March ground squirrels peep out of their holes, and bluebirds have also shown themselves. Robins make their appearance all the way from the first week in March to the first week in April. But some of them linger with us on winter half pay through the cold season. Sparrows, blackbirds, phœbe birds, wild pigeons drop in during the month. A few flies, a grasshopper, a butterfly, a snake, a turtle may be met with.

A flock of wild geese wedging their way northward, with strange far-off clamor, are the heralds of April. In another week the frogs begin piping. Toads and tree toads, martins and swallows, straggle along in through this month, or make themselves seen or heard in May.

The flowers are opening fast in the last part of April. Before May Day Mr. Higginson has found bloodroot, cowslip, dandelion, chickweed, strawberry, bellwort, dogtooth violet, five species of violet proper, to say nothing of some rarer plants than these. The leaves are springing bright green upon the currant bushes; dark, almost livid upon the lilac; the grass is growing apace, the plants are coming up in the garden beds, and the children are thinking of May Day.

The birds come pouring in with May. Wrens, brown thrushes, the various kinds of swallows, orioles, catbirds, golden robins, bobolinks, whippoorwills, cuckoos, yellowbirds, humming birds are busy in establishing their new households. The bumblebee comes in with his "mellow, breezy bass," to swell the song of the busy minstrels.

May is the flowering month of the orchard. As the warmth flows northward like a great wave, it covers the land with an ever-spreading flood of pink and white blossoms—the flowers of the peach, the cherry, the apple, and other fruit trees.

June comes in with roses in her hand, but very often with a thick shawl on her shoulders, and a bad cold in her head. But now the roses are coming into bloom; the azalea, wild honeysuckle, is sweetening the roadsides; the laurels are beginning to blow; the white lilies are getting ready to open; the fireflies are seen now and then flitting across the darkness; the katydids, the grasshoppers, the crickets make themselves heard; the bullfrogs utter their tremendous voices, and the full chorus of the birds makes the air vocal with its melody.

The flowering meadows are so sweet during the first week of July that the ailanthus thinks it must try to do better. It tries and fails ignominiously. In the garden the stately hollyhock is practicing the same economy. Is anything more charming in its way, than an old-fashioned single hollyhock, with its pink or white or yellow or purple flower, and the little pollen-powdered tree springing up from the bottom of the corolla? A bee should be buzzing in it, for a bee is never so deliciously pavilioned as in the bell tent of the hollyhock.

The saddest days of the year have not yet come, but the goldenrod and the aster have been long in bloom on the hill and in the wood, and by the roadside. The birds have been already consulting about their departure for the South. The foliage has been losing its freshness through the month of August, and here and there a yellow leaf shows itself like the first gray hair amidst the locks of a beauty who has seen one season too many. The evenings have become decidedly cooler than those of midsummer.

The world is getting to feel rich, for his golden fruits are ripening fast, and he has a large balance in the barns, which are his banks. September is dressing herself in showy dahlias and splendid marigolds and starry zinnias. October, the extravagant sister, has ordered an immense amount of the most gorgeous forest tapestry for her grand reception.

Thanksgiving is the winding up of autumn. The leaves are off the trees, except here and there on a beech or an oak; there is nothing left on the boughs but a few nuts and empty birds' nests. The earth looks desolate, and it will be a comfort to have the

snow on the ground, and to hear the merry jingle of
the sleigh bells.   —Oliver Wendell Holmes

1. How can you tell that Mr. Holmes loved nature?
   Where do you think he spent much of his time?
2. Do parts of the selection make you think of
   any poems you have studied?
3. Explain the first part of the sixth paragraph.
4. Describe pictures that might be used to illustrate each paragraph.
5. Mr. Holmes lived in New England, where the
   coming of spring is often late. Are the conditions he mentions different in your state?
6. What trees, flowers, or birds that he refers to
   do you not have? What kinds do you have that
   he does not mention?
7. Copy from this selection, in separate lists, the
   names of birds, insects, flowers, trees.
8. Give the meaning of "linger," "clamor,"
   "heralds," "tapestry," "desolate," "minstrels,"
   "ignominiously."

LESSON 259

REVIEW

1. Copy from Lesson 258: six pronouns, fifteen
   adjectives, fifteen verbs.
2. Write after each pronoun its antecedent.

LESSON 260

SENTENCES LIKE MODEL

1. Copy the first sentence in Lesson 258. Using it as a model, complete the following sentences:
   A. As late as the last of October _____.
   B. As early in the summer as _____.
   C. As early as the first of November _____.
   D. As late as the middle of April _____.
   Let the sentences be about insects, flowers, birds, fruits, or the coming of the snow.
2. Write sentences containing the following expressions: "heralds of spring," "flowering meadows," "saddest days of the year," "gorgeous tapestry."

LESSON 261

QUOTATIONS

People often keep notebooks in which they write beautiful quotations.

1. Select quotations of poetry or prose that especially please you. Read them and tell why you like them. Copy them in your notebook and add to them the best quotations that other members of the class read. Select quotations that are not given in this book.

LESSON 262

SELECTION TO BE MEMORIZED

THE YEAR'S AT THE SPRING

> The year's at the spring
> And day's at the morn;
> Morning's at seven;
> The hillside's dew-pearled;
> The lark's on the wing;
> The snail's on the thorn
> God's in his heaven—
> All's right with the world!

—ROBERT BROWNING

This stanza is taken from "Pippa Passes." Pippa was a poor girl who worked in the silk mills, and had only one holiday in the whole year. On the morning of the holiday she passed down the street singing this song.

1. What time of the year is described?
2. What time of day?
3. What shows that Pippa was contented?
4. What contractions do you find in the poem?
5. Memorize the stanza.
6. Write the stanza from memory.

LESSON 263

ADVERBS

A. The ground squirrels peep timidly out of their holes.

B. The flowers will blossom soon.

C. Beautiful trees grow here.

1. What is the verb in the first sentence? What word modifies the meaning of the verb by telling *how?*

2. What is the verb in the second sentence? What word modifies the meaning of the verb by telling *when?*

3. What is the verb in the third sentence? What word modifies the meaning of the verb by telling *where?*

Note: A word that modifies a verb is an *adverb*.

4. Add to each of the following sentences adverbs that tell *how:*

A. The bluebirds are singing.

B. The brook murmurs.

C. The child plays.

D. The fire burns.

E. The dog barks.

F. The children did their work.

G. The lion roared.

5. Use these adverbs in sentences: *quietly, patiently, kindly, quickly, carefully, fiercely, roughly, loudly, carelessly.*

6. Use these adverbs in sentences: *often, seldom, daily, yearly, early, late, always, soon, never.*

7. Use these adverbs in sentences: *there, here, down, up, backward, forward.*

8. Which adverbs tell *how?*

9. Which adverbs tell *when?*

10. Which adverbs tell *where?*

LESSON 264

ADVERBS—Continued

A. We crossed a high mountain.

B. We crossed a very high mountain.

1. What adjective do you find in the first sentence?

2. In the second sentence what word modifies the adjective?

Note: A word that modifies an adjective is an *adverb.*

3. Copy the following adverbs and place an adjective after each: *too, so, quite, very, more, most, less, least.*

4. Use in sentences the expressions you have formed.

LESSON 265

ADVERBS—Continued

A. You must listen carefully.

B. You must listen more carefully.

1. What adverb do you find in the first sentence?

2. In sentence B what word modifies the adverb?
Note: A word that modifies another adverb is an *adverb*.

3. Copy the following words, and place a suitable adverb after each: *very, more, least, quite, too.*

4. Use in sentences the expressions formed.

5. Complete the following definition:
An adverb is a word that modifies a verb ,
an _____, or another _____.

LESSON 266

COMPOSITION

1. Bring to school business circulars, or advertisements clipped from papers.

2. What special points must be observed in writing such articles?

3. Write an article suitable for a circular advertising the business of one of the following: *grocer, plumber, florist, dry goods merchant, jeweler.*

LESSON 267

SELECTION FOR STUDY—A BIOGRAPHY

SAMUEL MORSE

The well known American inventor, Samuel Morse, was born at Charlestown, Massachusetts, April 27, 1791, and he died in New York, New York, April 2, 1872. He attended the common schools of his native town and then entered Yale College, from which he was graduated in 1810. It was here that he first studied chemistry, galvanism, and electricity.

After his graduation Mr. Morse decided to be an artist. He went to London and studied for four years at the Royal Academy. He was quite successful and he received several prizes and other honors. Returning to America he became a popular portrait painter, first in Boston and later in Charleston, South Carolina.

Again he went abroad to study, and on the return voyage he met a Mr. Jackson, who had been studying electricity in Paris, and who told him of some recent experiments by the French in which electricity had been transmitted long distances and said, "How fine it would be if news could be sent in this way!"

Mr. Morse replied, "Why can't it be?"

During the remainder of the voyage the artist spent his time in drawing plans for apparatus and in trying to devise an alphabet.

After three years he completed his first model of a recording instrument, and two years later, in 1837, he put two of his instruments at the ends of a short line and received and sent messages. That same year he applied for a patent and asked for an appropriation from Congress to build a trial line from Washington to Baltimore. The next six years were spent in trying to get recognition and help in both Europe and the United States, during which time Mr. Morse often suffered for the common necessities of life.

Finally the line from Baltimore to Washington was completed and exhibited to a crowd of interested spectators. The test was successful, and companies were formed for the erection of telegraph lines in all parts of the United States.

Because of his inventions and the benefits that they conferred upon mankind, Mr. Morse received many honors both at home and abroad.

1. Tell what you can of the way in which messages are transmitted.
2. Of what value is the telegraph?
3. Why did Mr. Morse want a patent on his invention? What kinds of things are patented?
4. What protection does the government give the author of a book?
5. Find in this book the mark of the copyright.
6. Tell the story of the invention of the telegraph.

LESSON 268

TELEGRAMS

1. Tell what you can about telegrams.
2. Why are telegrams sent instead of letters?
3. If you wish to send a telegram, where would you take it?
4. Write telegrams for the following, so that each will contain not more than ten words besides the address and signature:

   A. To a relative who lives in another city— your mother and yourself will arrive on the six o'clock train, Saturday morning; ask the relative to meet you at the train; mention the name of the railroad.

   B. To a dealer in bicycles in another city— order a boy's or girl's bicycle; state the make wanted; ask that it be shipped at once by freight or express.

   C. To someone in the country, or a small town, asking him to ship fruit to a store in the city: state the price that will be paid, and the quantity wanted.

LESSON 269

PREPOSITIONS

1. Read again the first paragraph of Lesson 267. What word shows the relation of *Charlestown* to the other part of the sentence? What word shows the relation of *New York* to the other part of the sentence? What word shows the relation of *his native town* to the other part of the sentence?

Note: A word that shows the relation of a noun or something used as a noun to the rest of the sentence is called a *preposition*.

2. Copy five prepositions from Lesson 267.

3. Use the following prepositions in sentences:

A. about	G. before	M. except	S. behind
B. for	H. till	N. above	T. below
C. from	I. to	O. across	U. beneath
D. in	J. into	P. toward	V. after
E. beside	K. against	Q. of	W. on
F. under	L. between	R. with	X. over

LESSON 270

COMPOSITION—A BIOGRAPHY

1. Make an outline from Lesson 267.

Note: The written history of a person's life is called a *biography*.

2. How does a biography differ from an autobiography?
3. Write a short biography of one of the following: *George Washington, Abraham Lincoln, the President of the United States, an author, an artist, a prominent man in your neighborhood.*

LESSON 271

CORRECT USE OF WORDS

1. Write questions beginning with the following: *of whom, with whom, for whom, by whom, to whom, from whom.*
Note: The word *who* is never used after a preposition.
2. Write five questions beginning with *Who*.
3. Write questions which the following statements might answer; begin each question with *Whom*. As,
   A. Samuel Morse met a friend on the ship.
   B. Whom did Samuel Morse meet on the ship?
   C. The people praised Michael Angelo.
   D. Millet loved the poor people.
   E. The Pilgrims feared the Indians.
   F. Echo laughed at Juno.
   G. The teacher praised the industrious pupils.
   H. I saw many friends at the park.
   I. I took my brother for a ride.

LESSON 272

SELECTION FOR STUDY

The Coming of Spring

There's something in the air
That's new and sweet and rare—
A scent of summer things,
A whir as if of wings.

There's something, too, that's new
In color of the blue
That's in the morning sky,
Before the sun is high.

And though on plain and hill
'Tis winter, winter still,
There's something seems to say
That winter's had its day.

And all this changing tint,
This whispering stir, and hint
Of bud and bloom and wing,
Is the coming of the spring.

And tomorrow or today
The brooks will break away
From their icy, frozen sleep,
And run, and laugh, and leap!

And the next thing, in the woods,
The catkins in their hoods
Of fur and silk will stand,
A sturdy little band.

And the tassels soft and fine
Of the hazel will entwine,
And the elder branches show
Their buds against the snow.

So, silently but swift,
Above the wintry drift,
The long days gain and gain,
Until, on hill and plain—

Once more, and yet once more,
Returning as before,
We see the bloom of birth
Make young again the earth.

—NORA PERRY

1. What month does this poem suggest?
2. Use in sentences: "morning sky," "changing tint," "frozen sleep," "wintry sky."
3. Copy from the poem four contractions, and write with each its equivalent.
4. Memorize the part of the poem that you like best.

LESSON 273

SELECTION FOR STUDY

A bird's real home is the place where he is seen in summer and where he brings up his family. He travels in winter for pleasure—the pleasure of eating; for, if he is a winter traveler, you may be sure that his kind of food is not to be found at that season in the place which he calls his home.

Nothing but the need of food, or cold too severe for them to endure, could ever induce the birds to leave the place they love better than any other in the whole world.

They prove themselves home lovers by returning to the same place year after year. Some even nest in the same tree or repair the same old nest in which they were so contented. Never once would they think of going to housekeeping or bringing up families in that land so far away.

Though they appear to be perfectly free to do as they choose, living only for pleasure, they are really the most industrious little bodies to be found anywhere.

Imagine yourself just getting home from the far South and having to go to work immediately to build a house, every scrap of which you would have to search for and carry to the building spot. Imagine yourself having to hunt for every mouthful of food, with that same food all the time trying to get away from you.

Then think of yourself, later in the season, as having to get a meal for a hungry family of little ones, every five or ten minutes, sometimes as often as every two minutes. I wonder if you would be as cheerful, through it all, as they.

—FROM *OUR BIRDS AND THEIR NESTLINGS*

1. Copy in separate lists, from the selection:

    A. nouns   C. pronouns   E. adjectives

    B. verbs   D. adverbs   F. prepositions

2. Copy the first paragraph, so changed that each of the nouns and pronouns will mean more than one.

3. What verbs was it necessary to change? What verbs add *s* when the subject means only one? What change did you make in the possessive form?

4. What is the central thought in each paragraph?

5. Make an outline of this selection.

6. Close the book and, using the outline you have made, reproduce as much as you can of the thought of the author.

7. Find a sentence in the transposed order.

8. Name the subject of each sentence in the third paragraph.

LESSON 274

SELECTION TO BE MEMORIZED

THE FLAG GOES BY

Hats off!
Along the street there comes
A blare of bugles, a ruffle of drums,
A flash of color beneath the sky:
Hats off!
The flag is passing by!
Blue and crimson and white it shines,
Over the steel-tipped, ordered lines.
Hats off!
The colors before us fly;
But more than the flag is passing by.
Sea fights and land fights, grim and great,
Fought to make and save the State:
Weary marches and sinking ships;
Cheers of victory on dying lips;
Days of plenty and years of peace;
March of a strong land's swift increase;
Equal justice, right, and law,
Stately honor and reverend awe:
Sign of a nation, great and strong
To ward her people from foreign wrong;
Pride and glory and honor—all
Live in the colors to stand or fall.

Hats off!
Along the street there comes
A blare of bugles, a ruffle of drums;
And loyal hearts are beating high:
Hats off !
The flag is passing by!

—HENRY H. BENNETT

1. Why the command "Hats off"?
2. Explain "blare of bugles."
3. What do you understand by "steel-tipped lines"?
4. Explain the last line of the second stanza.
5. What are mentioned in the third, fourth, and fifth stanzas, as living in the colors of the flag?
6. Memorize the poem.
7. Write the first and second stanzas from memory.

LESSON 275

DICTATION

A thoughtful mind, when it sees a nation's flag, sees not the flag only, but the nation itself; and whatever may be its symbols, its insignia, he reads chiefly in the flag the government, the principles, the truths, the history, which belong to the nation which sets it forth.

—HENRY WARD BEECHER

1. Write the paragraph from dictation.
2. Write a list of the nouns in the paragraph.
3. Write a list of the verbs.

LESSON 276

CONVERSATION—THE SOLDIER

1. Tell what you can of the life of a soldier.
2. What kind of uniform does he wear?
3. What are his duties in time of peace?
4. Name some of the titles of officers of the United States army. Who is highest in command? How is the rank of an officer indicated by his uniform?
5. Explain the following terms:

A. artillery   E. cavalry   I. infantry
B. commissary   F. department   J. barracks
C. rations   G. fortications   K. flag of truce
D. captain   H. corporal   L. lieutenant

6. When is a city said to be besieged?
7. When is an army said to be intrenched?
8. How are the wounded cared for?
9. Of what use is the bayonet?
10. What are the duties of a scout?
11. Why is it necessary to keep a standing army in time of peace?
12. Where is the national military school located?

LESSON 277

SELECTION FOR STUDY

A MAN WITHOUT A COUNTRY

Edward Everett Hale has written a story about an army officer who once in his anger wished that he might never again hear the name of the United States. As his punishment, his wish was granted. He passed the remainder of his life upon war vessels, where he was treated with kindness, but where no one was allowed to speak to him of his country, nor was he allowed to read a paper or magazine that in any way referred to it.

At first the punishment seemed light, but as the years passed, his desire to hear of his country grew almost greater than he could bear.

The following words he once spoke to a young sailor on the ship:

"For your country, boy, and for that flag, never dream a dream but of serving her as she bids you, though the service carry you through a thousand terrors. No matter what happens to you, no matter who flatters you or who abuses you, never look at another flag, never let a night pass but you pray God to bless that flag. Remember, boy, that behind all these men you have to deal with, behind officers, and government, and people even, there is the Country Herself, your

Country, and that you belong to Her as you do to your own mother. Stand by Her, boy, as you would stand by your mother."

1. Read this several times. Tell the incident, and repeat as much as you can of the paragraph quoted.
2. If possible read the book, *A Man without a Country.*

LESSON 278

CONJUNCTIONS

1. In Lesson 277 what words does *or* connect?
2. In the second paragraph what does *but* connect?
3. In the fourth paragraph what does *and* connect?
   Note: A word that connects words, sentences, or parts of sentences is called a *conjunction.*
4. Write a sentence in which *and* connects two or more words.
5. Write a sentence in which *and* connects parts of sentences or whole sentences.
6. Write a sentence in which *but* connects two sentences.
7. Write a sentence in which *or* connects words.
8. Write a sentence in which *or* connects sentences or parts of sentences.

LESSON 279

COMPOSITION—THE FLAG

1. Find out something concerning the history of our flag; tell by whom the first flag was made.
2. Describe the flag. How many stripes has it? What is the historical significance of the stripes?
3. How many stars are there now in the blue field? How has this number been changed?
4. For what does the flag stand? What feelings should the sight of it rouse in every citizen of the United States?
5. Write a short composition on "The Flag of the United States."

LESSON 280

CONVERSATION

1. Who is governor of your state?
2. To what political party does he belong?
3. Mention some of his duties.
4. For how long a term is he elected?
5. When does his present term expire?
6. By whom are the laws of your state made?
7. Tell something about the legislature.
8. How are the expenses of the state government paid?

LESSON 281

INTERJECTIONS

A. Soldiers, awake!

B. Hark! I hear the bugles and drums.

C. Hurrah! The soldiers are coming.

1. What words in the sentences above are used to address, to attract attention, or to express feeling? **Note: A word used by itself to address, to attract attention, or to express feeling is called an *interjection*. It is not to be regarded as a part of a sentence, but as an independent word. The interjection is usually followed by an exclamation point.**

2. Write sentences containing the following words used as interjections:

A. what   C. behold   E. alas   G. good

B. oh   D hark   F. pshaw   H. hurrah

Note: The interjection *O* should always be written with a capital. It is used with a noun denoting the person or thing spoken to. It is not followed by any special mark of punctuation. As,

O Mother   O God

Oh **is an interjection of surprise, joy, or grief. It is usually followed by a comma. As,**

Oh, I am so sorry!

LESSON 282

SELECTION FOR STUDY

COLUMBUS

Behind him lay the gray Azores,
  Behind the Gates of Hercules;
Before him not the ghost of shores,
  Behind him only shoreless seas.
The good mate said, "Now must we pray,
  For lo! The very stars are gone.
Brave Admiral, speak, what shall I say?"
  "Why, say, 'Sail on! Sail on! And on!'"

"My men grow mutinous day by day;
  My men grow ghastly wan and weak."
The stout mate thought of home; a spray
  Of salt wave washed his swarthy cheek.
"What shall I say, brave Admiral, say,
  If we sight naught but seas at dawn?"
"Why, you shall say at break of day,
  'Sail on! Sail on! Sail on! And on!'"

They sailed and sailed, as winds might blow,
  Until at last the blanched mate said,
"Why, now not even God would know
  Should I and all my men fall dead.

These very winds forget their way,
  For God from these dread seas is gone.
Now speak, brave Admiral, speak and say—"
  He said, "Sail on! Sail on! And on!"

They sailed. They sailed. Then spake the mate:
  "This mad sea shows his teeth tonight.
He curls his lip, he lies in wait,
  With lifted teeth, as if to bite!
Brave Admiral, say but one good word;
  What shall we do when hope is gone?"
The words leaped like a raging sword:
  "Sail on! Sail on! Sail on! And on!"

Then, pale and worn, he kept his deck,
  And peered through darkness. Ah, that night
Of all dark nights! And then a speck—
  A light! A light! A light! A light!
It grew, a starlit flag unfurled!
  It grew to be Time's burst of dawn.
He gained a world; he gave that world
  Its grandest lesson: "On! Sail on!"

—JOAQUIN MILLER

1. Find in the dictionary the meaning of "mutinous,"
"ghastly," "swarthy," "blanched," "naught."

2. Who was the Admiral?
3. Where are the Azores?
4. What reasons did the mate give for wishing to turn back?
5. What is meant by "shoreless seas"?
6. Who speaks the words in the last line of the first stanza?
7. Explain lines one and two of the second stanza.
8. Read the words of Columbus, in the second stanza.
9. Why did they sail "as winds might blow"?
10. What is the meaning of lines two, three, and four in the fourth stanza?
11. Why was the fear of the sailors so great?
12. Give in your own words the thought in the fifth stanza.
13. Try to imagine the scene on the ship when a light on shore was discovered. Describe what may have happened.
14. Read what Columbus said in the first stanza. Find the *quotation within the quotation.*
Note: Notice that it is enclosed in single marks (' '). Find in the second stanza a quotation within a quotation.
15. Memorize the stanza that you like best.

LESSON 283

PICTURE STUDY—COLUMBUS

Tell what you can of the points suggested in the following outline:

1. Before the discovery of America what did most people believe about the shape of the earth? What did Columbus believe?
2. What did Columbus wish to find?
3. Why did he have difficulty in securing aid?
4. Who helped him finally?
5. How many ships was he given?
6. Tell something of the voyage.
7. Why were the men afraid?
8. What were the first signs of land?
9. What were some of the things that Columbus and his men found in the new world?
10. Describe the picture showing his return to the court of Spain.
11. What are some of the things that you can imagine Columbus told the king?
12. What effect did his words have upon the king and the people who heard?
13. What did Columbus carry back with him from the new world?

From a painting by Brozik

COLUMBUS AT THE COURT OF FERDINAND AND ISABELLA

LESSON 284

SELECTION FOR STUDY

To lay down the pen and even to think of that beautiful Rhineland makes one happy. At this time of summer evenings, the cows are trooping down from the hills, lowing and with their bells tinkling, to the old town, with its old moats, and gates and spires, and chestnut trees, with long blue shadows stretching over the grass; the sky and the river below flame in crimson and gold, and the moon is already out looking pale toward the sunset. The sun sinks suddenly behind the great castle-crested mountains, the night falls quickly, the river grows darker and darker, lights quiver in it from the windows of the old ramparts, and twinkle peacefully in the villages under the hills on the opposite shore.

—WILLIAM MAKEPEACE THACKERAY

1. This paragraph describes the close of day. Using this as a model, write a description of the break of day.
    A. Begin in this way: The sun rises suddenly from behind the great castle-crested mountains _____.
    B. Tell how the dewdrops glisten, how the river grows brighter and brighter, and how the birds sing their morning songs. Tell how the cattle go out to the hills, and the men start to work in the fields.

LESSON 285

WORDS DERIVED FROM PROPER NOUNS

A. Japanese lanterns are made of paper.

B. French toys are expensive.

1. From what proper noun is the word *Japanese* derived?

2. From what proper noun is the word *French* derived?

3. With what kind of letter do words derived from proper nouns begin?

4. Name the proper nouns from which the following words are derived:

A. Russian	E. German	I. English
B. British	F. Portuguese	J. Irish
C. Scotch	G. Italian	K. Spanish
D. Mexican	H. Norwegian	

5. Use the words in sentences.

LESSON 286

INVITATIONS

FORMAL INVITATION

A. Mrs. John Fuller requests the pleasure of your company at a musicale, to be given at her home on Thursday, June the tenth, at eight o'clock.

ACCEPTANCE

B. Mrs. George Davis accepts with pleasure the kind invitation of Mrs. John Fuller for Thursday evening, June the tenth.

REGRET

C. Mrs. George Davis regrets that absence from the city will prevent her acceptance of Mrs. John Fuller's kind invitation for Thursday evening, June the tenth.

1. Study these forms.
2. Write a formal invitation to a party.
3. Write the acceptance which a friend might send.
4. Write a note regretting your inability to accept the invitation which a friend has sent you.
5. Write a formal invitation from the school for Patrons' Day.

LESSON 287

LETTER WRITING

T. L. Barnes, grocer, 1820 Main Street, St. Paul, MN, writes to George L. Owens, asking him to settle his account which is overdue.

1. Write the letter in a courteous way.

LESSON 288

SELECTION FOR STUDY—MAY

There came a message to the vine,
  A whisper to the tree;
The bluebird saw the secret sign
  And merrily sang he!
And like a silver string the brook
  Trembled with music sweet—
Enchanting notes in every nook
  For echo to repeat.

A magic touch transformed the fields,
  Greener each hour they grew,
Until they shone like burnished shields
  All jeweled o'er with dew.
Scattered upon the forest floor
  A million bits of bloom
Breathed fragrance forth thro' morning's door
  Into the day's bright room.

Then inch by inch the vine confessed
  The secret it had heard,
And in the leaves the azure breast
  Sang the delightful word:
Glad flowers upsprang amid the grass
  And flung their banners gay,
And suddenly it came to pass—
  God's Miracle of May!

—FRANK DEMPSTER SHERMAN

1. Use in sentences:
   A. secret sign B. enchanting notes C. magic touch
   D. amid the grass E. transformed F. confessed
   G. miracle H. burnished
2. Write three questions about the first stanza.
3. Write two questions about the second stanza.
4. Write two questions about the third stanza.

LESSON 289

CONVERSATION

1. Who is President of the United States?
2. To what political party does he belong?
3. For how long a term was he elected?
4. When does his present term expire?
5. What are some of his duties?
6. Who is Vice President of the United States?
7. Who makes the laws of the United States?
8. Of what two parts is Congress composed?
9. What are some of the duties of Congress?
10. How are the expenses of the Government paid?

LESSON 290

QUOTATIONS

1. Bring quotations and stories to illustrate the
   following subjects: A. obedience B. cleanliness
   C. promptness D. honesty.

LESSON 291

SELECTION FOR STUDY

DAFFODILS

I wander'd lonely as a cloud
    That floats on high o'er vales and hills,
When all at once I saw a crowd,
    A host of golden daffodils;
Beside the lake, beneath the trees,
Fluttering and dancing in the breeze.

Continuous as the stars that shine
    And twinkle on the Milky Way,
They stretched in never-ending line
    Along the margin of the bay:
Ten thousand saw I at a glance,
Tossing their heads in sprightly dance.

The waves beside them danced; but they
    Outdid the sparkling waves in glee;
A poet could not but be gay,
    In such a jocund company:
I gazed—and gazed—but little thought
What wealth the show to me had brought.

For oft, when on my couch I lie
    In vacant or in pensive mood,
They flash upon that inward eye
    Which is the bliss of solitude;

And then my heart with pleasure fills
And dances with the daffodils.

—WILLIAM WORDSWORTH

1. Give the meaning of: A. jocund B. continuous C. sprightly D. margin E. solitude F. vales.
2. Give synonyms for glee, wealth, bliss.
3. Explain the first and second lines of the first stanza.
4. What is the "Milky Way?"
5. In the second paragraph find an example of transposed order.
6. What do you understand by the last line of the third stanza?
7. What meaning do you find in the last stanza?
8. Describe the picture which the poem presents.

LESSON 292

SELECTION FOR STUDY

SUMMER RAIN

A good summer rain is a rain of riches. If gold and silver rattled down from the clouds, they could hardly enrich the land so much as soft, long rains. Every drop is silver going to the mint. The roots are machinery, and, catching the willing drops, they array them, refine them, stamp them, and turn them out coined berries, apples, grains, and grasses!

When the heavens send clouds and they bank up the horizon, be sure they have hidden gold in them. All the mountains of California are not so rich as are the soft mines of heaven, that send down treasures upon man without tasking him, and pour riches upon his field without spade or pickax—without his search or notice.

Well, let it rain, then! No matter if the journey is delayed, the picnic spoiled, the visit adjourned. Blessed be rain—and rain in summer. And blessed be He who watereth the earth and enricheth it for man and beast.

—HENRY WARD BEECHER

1. In the first paragraph what is compared to the coinage of money?
2. To what are the roots compared?
3. In the second paragraph to what are the clouds compared?
4. In the last paragraph why does *He* begin with a capital?
5. Write the first paragraph from dictation.
6. Use in sentences: A. *when the heavens send clouds* B. *the mountains of California* C. *a rain of riches* D. *every drop is silver* E. *the soft mines of heaven* F. *summer rain* G. *hidden gold.*

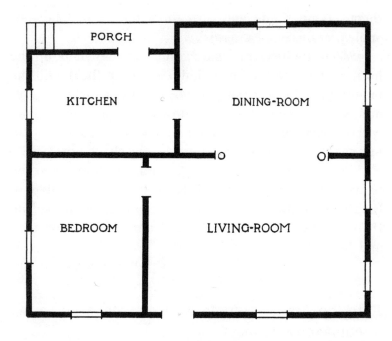

LESSON 293

DESCRIPTION—PLAN OF A HOUSE

1. Here is a plan for a house of four rooms. Draw a plan for a larger house.
2. Write a description of your plan.
3. In your description, give the size of each room, the number of windows, and the color of wall paper to be used.
4. State how each room is to be furnished.

LESSON 294

SELECTION TO BE MEMORIZED

Home, Sweet Home

'Mid pleasures and palaces though we may roam,
Be it ever so humble, there's no place like home!
A charm from the skies seems to hallow us there,
Which, seek through the world, is ne'er met with
    elsewhere.
    Home, home, sweet, sweet home!
    There's no place like home! There's no place
    like home!

An exile from home, splendor dazzles in vain;
Oh, give me my lonely thatched cottage again!
The birds singing gayly, that came at my call—
Oh, give me them—and the peace of mind, dearer
    than all!
    Home, home, sweet, sweet home!
    There's no place like home! There's no place
    like home!
              —John Howard Payne

1. Explain the second line of the first stanza. What does the third line mean?
2. Explain the first line of the second stanza.
3. Have you ever been anywhere and longed for home?
4. What is meant by "peace of mind"?

LESSON 295

LETTER WRITING

Frank Darby has applied for a position in a wholesale furniture store.

The manager, C. S. Ferguson, writes to Prof. Charles Barnes, principal of the _____ School, telling him that Frank has applied for a position, and asking if Professor Barnes can recommend his former pupil.   .

1. Write the letter. Use any city you wish in the heading.
2. Write the reply of Professor Barnes, telling of Frank's good habits, his promptness, his honesty, and other good points which an employer might wish to know.
    A. Begin the body of the letter in this way: Your letter of the _____ was received today. Frank Darby was a pupil in my school for six years _____.
3. Write another reply to the first letter saying that Professor Barnes regrets that he cannot recommend Frank Darby for the position in the furniture store. State why.

LESSON 296

CONVERSATION

1. Study these proverbs; what does each one teach? If possible, give stories or incidents to illustrate them.

A. Necessity is the mother of invention.
Suggestion for story: A boy who wishes to have a wagon but has no money to buy one.

B. Vinegar catches no flies.
Suggestion for story: A merchant who is cross and discourteous to all who enter his store.

C. A word to the wise is sufficient.

D. God helps them that help themselves.

E. Experience is a good teacher.

F. A bird in the hand is worth two in the bush.

G. A stitch in time saves nine.

H. All work and no play makes Jack a dull boy.

I. All is not gold that glitters.

J. A rolling stone gathers no moss.

K. It is never too late to mend.

L. An ounce of prevention is worth a pound of cure.

2. Write one of the stories.

LESSON 297

SELECTION FOR STUDY

THE DAY IS DONE

The day is done, and the darkness
    Falls from the wings of Night,
As a feather is wafted downward
    From an eagle in its flight.

I see the lights of the village
    Gleam through the rain and mist,
And a feeling of sadness comes o'er me
    That my soul cannot resist—

A feeling of sadness and longing,
    That is not akin to pain,
And resembles sorrow only
    As the mist resembles the rain.

Come, read to me some poem,
    Some simple and heartfelt lay,
That shall soothe this restless feeling,
    And banish the thoughts of day.

Not from the grand old masters,
    Not from the bards sublime,
Whose distant footsteps echo
    Through the corridors of Time.

For like strains of martial music,
　　Their mighty thoughts suggest
Life's endless toil and endeavor;
　　And tonight I long for rest.

Read from some humbler poet,
　　Whose songs gushed from his heart,
As showers from the clouds of summer,
　　Or tears from the eyelids start.

Who through long days of labor,
　　And nights devoid of ease,
Still heard in his soul the music
　　Of wonderful melodies.

Such songs have power to quiet
　　The restless pulse of care,
And come like the benediction
　　That follows after prayer.

Then read from the treasured volume
　　The poem of thy choice,
And lend to the rhyme of the poet
　　The beauty of thy voice.

And the night shall be filled with music,
　　And the cares that infest the day
Shall fold their tents, like the Arabs,
　　And as silently steal away.

　　　　　　　　—HENRY WADSWORTH LONGFELLOW

1. In the first stanza to what is the falling of darkness compared?
   Note: Such a comparison is called a *simile*. A simile usually is introduced by the words *as* or *like*.
2. Find a simile in the third stanza. What are compared?
3. Explain the third stanza. What is the meaning of "akin"?
4. Find a simile in the seventh paragraph. What are compared?
5. Read the fourth stanza. If such a request were made of you, what would you select to read? Mention one of the poets referred to in the sixth stanza.
6. Which stanza pleases you most?
8. Define and use in sentences these words:

   A. wafted   D. resist   G. resembles
   B. banish   E. bards   H. corridors
   C. martial   F. devoid   I. endeavor
9. Who wrote the poem?
10. Mention some other poems that Longfellow wrote.
11. Memorize this poem.
12. Copy sentences containing similes, from Lessons 169, 236, and 241.

LESSON 298

SELECTIONS FOR STUDY

1. Discuss the following selections in class; write the first one from dictation:

   A. We were not sent into this world to do anything into which we cannot put our hearts. We have certain work to do for our bread, and that is to be done strenuously; other work to do for our delight, and that is to be done heartily; neither is it to be done by halves or shifts, but with a will; and what is not worth this effort is not to be done at all.

   —JOHN RUSKIN

THE FOOTPATH TO PEACE

   B. To be glad of life, because it gives you the chance to love and to work and to play and to look up at the stars; to be satisfied with your possessions, but not contented with yourself until you have made the best of them; to despise nothing in the world except falsehood and meanness, and to fear nothing except cowardice; to covet nothing that is your neighbor's except his kindness of heart and gentleness of manners; and to spend as much time as you can, with body and with spirit, in God's out-of-doors. These are little guideposts on the footpath to peace.

   —HENRY VAN DYKE

LESSON 299

SUGGESTIONS FOR DESCRIPTIONS

1. Write a description of a pleasant bedroom. Tell about the wall paper, windows and curtains, the furniture, and the good order in which it is kept. Make your description so clear that others will see the picture as you do.

2. Write a description of an untidy dining room. Tell about the things that make it unattractive.

3. Describe some building in your neighborhood without telling where or what it is. You should tell of its size compared with a church, its color, general shape, and the use to which it is put. Is it an ornament to the neighborhood?

4. Suppose that you have a large yard in which you wish to plant trees, ornamental shrubs, and flowers. Draw a diagram of the lot, showing location of house, flower beds, etc. Would you leave a space for a kitchen garden? What would you plant in it? Write a description of it as you would have it appear.

5. Write a description of some character in a book that you have read recently.

LESSON 300

SELECTION FOR STUDY

A few years ago the children of New York were asked to help keep the city clean. At a great meeting they sang the following song:

There are barrels in the hallways,
    Neighbor mine,
Pray be mindful of them always,
    Neighbor mine.
If you're not devoid of feeling,
Quickly to those barrels stealing,
Throw in each banana peeling,
    Neighbor mine.

    *   *   *   *   *

Paper cups were made for papers,
    Neighbor mine,
Let's not have the fact escape us,
    Neighbor mine.
And if you will lend a hand,
Soon our city dear shall stand
As the cleanest in the land,
    Neighbor mine.

—From *Town and City*

1. What is this poem intended to teach?
2. Write five rules for keeping streets, sidewalks, and yards in good condition.

LESSON 301

SUMMARY—Continued from Lesson 248

TO REMEMBER

A word that expresses action, being, or state of being is called a *verb*.

An *adverb* is a word that modifies a verb, an adjective, or another adverb.

A word that shows the relation of a noun or something used as a noun to the other part of the sentence is called a *preposition*.

A word that connects words, sentences, or parts of sentences is called a *conjunction*.

A word used by itself to address or call attention or express feeling is called an *interjection*.

A word derived from a proper noun begins with a capital letter.

To express simple future use *shall* with *I* and *we*; use *will* with all other words.

To express determination use *will* with *I* and *we*; use *shall* with all other words.

INDEX

Books Available from
Lost Classics Book Company
American History
Stories of Great Americans for Little Americans..Edward Eggleston
A First Book in American History .... Edward Eggleston
A History of the United States and Its People....... Edward Eggleston
Biography
The Life of Kit Carson..Edward Ellis
English Grammar
Primary Language Lessons ....Emma Serl
Intermediate Language Lessons .... Emma Serl
(Teacher's Guides Available for Both Textbooks)
Elson Readers Series
The Elson Readers: Primer......................William Elson, Lura Runkel
The Elson Readers: Book One ....William Elson, Lura Runkel
The Elson Readers: Book Two ....William Elson, Lura Runkel
The Elson Readers: Book Three .... William Elson
The Elson Readers: Book Four .... William Elson
The Elson Readers: Book Five ....William Elson, Christine Keck
The Elson Readers: Book Six ....William Elson, Christine Keck
The Elson Readers: Book Seven...........William Elson, Christine Keck
The Elson Readers: Book Eight.............William Elson, Christine Keck
(Teacher's Guides Available for Each Reader in This Series)
Historical Fiction
With Lee in Virginia..G. A. Henty
A Tale of the Western Plains .... G. A. Henty
The Young Carthaginian..G. A. Henty
In the Heart of the Rockies ....G. A. Henty
For the Temple ....G. A. Henty
A Knight of the White Cross ....G. A. Henty
The Minute Boys of Lexington........................ Edward Stratemeyer
The Minute Boys of Bunker Hill...................... Edward Stratemeyer
Hope and Have .... Oliver Optic
Taken by the Enemy, First in *The Blue and the Gray Series*...............Oliver Optic
Within the Enemy's Lines, Second in *The Blue and the Gray Series* ..Oliver Optic
On the Blockade, Third in *The Blue and the Gray Series*.....................Oliver Optic
Stand by the Union, Fourth in *The Blue and the Gray Series*..............Oliver Optic
Fighting for the Right, Fifth in *The Blue and the Gray Series*............Oliver Optic
A Victorious Union, Sixth and Final in *The Blue and the Gray Series*.....Oliver Optic
Mary of Plymouth ....James Otis
By Reef and Trail.. Fisher Ames, Jr.

For more information visit us at: http://www.lostclassicsbooks.com